D1050059

TWENTY
20th Century
JEWS

by

S. J. GOLDSMITH

Drawings by
JULIET PANNETT

Biography Index Reprint Series

BOOKS FOR LIBRARIES PRESS
FREEPORT, NEW YORK

STANDARD BOOK NUMBER:
8369-8000-X

LIBRARY OF CONGRESS CATALOG CARD NUMBER:
70-101827

PRINTED IN THE UNITED STATES OF AMERICA

Preface

Twenty Jews ranging from the Prime Minister of Israel to the co-discoverer of penicillin, from a promoter of chain stores to a great cartoonist, from a famous writer to a Socialist leader, from a high court judge to an archeologist, ought to give a fairly good picture of the outlets which the Jewish genius has found in the twentieth century. There is one claim that can be made on behalf of all the twenty — they are outstanding *as people* and not only as Jews. In fact, only two of them are "Jewish Jews;" all the others are Jews whose contribution and impact are of a universal nature. All the twenty, without exception, are humanists in the widest and noblest sense. There is not one in this group who is narrow-mindedly Jewish to the exclusion of all other interests and loyalties.

This is no accident. Another group of twenty eminent Jews would have presented a similar picture. It is part of the Jewish heritage.

When Lely painted Oliver Cromwell, he was told by his redoubtable sitter: "Remark all these roughnesses, pimples, warts and everything as you see me, otherwise I will never pay a farthing for it."

None of my "victims" addressed me in such terms. The modest ones simply inquired whether I must include them in the volume, and when I explained that I had not come to consult them about the list, they co-operated nicely. I tried myself to remember Cromwell's order to Lely, and to act upon it to the best of my ability.

One of the subjects in the book, for whose judgment and sagacity I have great respect, has written me to say that after reading his profile he felt it was like having his X-ray displayed in public. But he did not complain. Those in the public eye cannot both lose their privacy and have it. I trust the others will not complain either.

These essays must be looked upon as landscape paintings rather than detailed survey maps. Perhaps there is consolation in the fact that paintings invariably give more pleasure than survey maps — and, incidentally, fetch much higher prices.

Which brings me to my publisher, Mr. Moshe Sheinbaum, who is also a friend of long standing. I am greatly indebted to him for a number of valuable suggestions above and beyond those normally made by a publisher, and for taking so much trouble to produce an attractive volume.

Juliet Pannett, who did the drawings, tells me that she enjoyed her sessions with the sitters. Nevertheless, I know what great pains she took in tracking them down and keeping them still. The drawings are vintage Pannett, the work of one of the finest artists in this medium.

This is also an opportunity to express my thanks to my friends, William Frankel, editor of the London *Jewish Chronicle*, and Bernard Postal, editor of the American *Jewish Digest*, for their permission to use those of the profiles that have appeared in their journals as nuclei for the fuller treatment in the book.

The advice I have had from Mr. Bernard Reines, the editor for Shengold Publishers, Inc., is very much appreciated.

London, November, 1962   S. J. G.

CONTENTS

Twenty 20th Century Jews

D. Ben-Gurion

Juliet Pannett

David Ben-Gurion

The Maker of History

T HE DREAM OF ZION began to assume the shape of reality some eighty years ago. Slowly, yet surely, it developed sinews, grew flesh, covered itself with skin — like those dry bones in the vision of the Prophet Ezekiel. And all this time, Jews fondly speculated about the coming Jewish state and conjured up its image. What would it look like — a Jewish state with its own government, army, police, post office?

Liberated Jews told me after the war that during the darkest days in the ghettos and concentration camps they used to derive comfort from speculations about the coming Jewish state. Sometimes they would try to imagine its prime minister: Would he be like Disraeli? Or perhaps like Leon Blum? Or maybe somebody like Herzl? In the end somebody invariably suggested that, after all, there was no point in idle speculation: Weizmann was there, waiting to take office. Indeed, as the war drew to a close, many free Jews could also see him ruling in Jerusalem. But this was not to be. The figure of David Ben-Gurion emerged on the horizon, and Weizmann had to give way; he was earmarked for the exalted but powerless position of president, some two years before the state came into being.

Ben-Gurion staked his claim to the premiership at the twenty-first Zionist Congress at Basle, in December of 1946. There were no challengers. What was much more important, all the Jews, those in Palestine and those outside, guided by that sixth sense which never lets a people down, knew that Ben-Gurion was the right man to be the first prime minister of the Third Jewish Commonwealth.

Ben-Gurion himself accepted his destiny without humility. He seemed to think that the *Sar Haumah,* the Guardian Angel of the Jewish people, had entrusted him with the task, and that he was not only the best man we had, but the right man for the assignment; the man to tackle the difficulties, not only as well as could be expected, but really well by any yardstick, contemporary or historical — so well, in fact, that the historian of the future would have no cause for complaint. He may have been right, too.

It is said that the proper training for a British prime minister is Eton and Oxford, war service, the House of Commons, a couple of lesser officers in the Government and the Chancellorship of the Exchequer. For a French prime minister, they say, it is any high school, the École Normale Superiere, the mayorality of a provincial town, and the leadership of a political party. For an American president it seems to be Yale or Harvard, the Senate, and/or the governorship of one of the states of the Union, always making allowance for exceptions.

The training for the office of the first prime minister of Israel was, inevitably, an East-European background, physical work on reclamation of the land, the *Hashomer,* the Jewish Legion in the First World War, Zionist politics, self-education, and a leading position in the struggle for independence. If a committee had had to devise the curriculum, it would have had to draw it up along the lines of Ben-Gurion's life story. But it is, of course, the man that counts, and not his apprenticeship.

The historian of the future will, no doubt, rank David Ben-Gurion with Joshua, King David, and Judas Maccabeus. He will be compared with Washington, Churchill, Lenin. The legends are already being woven, and they will accumulate as time goes on. The bare facts, before the "miracles" took place, are arrival in in Palestine from Plonsk, Russian Poland, in 1906, at the age of twenty; pioneering work on the land; night watch on horseback; exile by the Turks; work on a farm in North Dakota; and campaigning in New York to recruit men for the Jewish Legion. The "miracles" (and here I doubt whether I should really use the quotation marks — it is the rational mind that makes them creep in) followed.

It is not open to argument that the main characteristic of Ben-Gurion's personality is moral courage, which was brought into play at the most decisive moments, in his own career and in the history of the Jewish people, with so much effect that it tipped the scales.

Moral courage in the person of Ben-Gurion is allied to a prophetic streak, which implies having not only the vision, but also the inner strength to proclaim it, which is another aspect of moral courage. In fact, moral courage is the hallmark of all true prophets. And like all the prophets, major and minor, he alternates between admonition, warning, comforting, and peering into the shrouded future.

One of my most vivid and moving memories of a period crowded with the events of the war and its aftermath, is Ben-Gurion's address to the liberated Jews of Belsen. I was a war correspondent in those days, and I chanced to arrive at the camp to look up some old friends while Ben-Gurion was paying them his first visit. It was November, 1945. He addressed a mass meeting and concluded his speech with a memorable peroration. Gripping his temples he exclaimed: "You see these grey hairs of mine — they will live to see a Jewish state in Eretz Israel."

There was very little evidence to justify such a forecast, but we all knew in our heart of hearts, we felt in our bones, that what he had just said was true, that it would come to pass.

Ben-Gurion was not, of course, picked out to take charge in 1946 just because he had an impressive head of grey hair. When Ben-Gurion came to the decisive Basle Congress, he had behind him not only the humdrum work of campaigning and negotiating; he had also been the chief architect — not the only one, but the most outstanding of a group — who gradually converted the peaceful, halutzic settlers and the meek town-dwellers into a movement of resistance and liberation. He was one of the few who prepared the state underground, so that it could be proclaimed on "I-Day."

And now the moral courage had to be summoned, and it was found to be sufficient. The situation was a paradoxical one. Ben-Gurion could not co-operate with his political adversaries in the *Yishuv*, the members of the Etzel and Lechi movements, who were ready, eager, and straining at the leash to proclaim the state. At the same time, his friends and collaborators were full of doubts, hesitations, fears, and forebodings. On the face of it, judged by normal standards, they seemed to be justified. The Haganah was untried as an army in the field. The Arabs outnumbered the Jews about forty to one. They had arms, and were thought to be stronger than they turned out to be. The pro-Arab policy of Britain was in full flower. The Americans were talking with two voices, that of the State Department and that of the White House, and no one could tell which of them would carry the day; no effective help could be expected from America. Russia was sympathetic, but help from her was neither desirable nor available. Worst of all, perhaps, most of the people in Ben-Gurion's own circle, his colleagues who were soon to become members of his Government, were shaky and hesitant. Some were not ready for the reality of a state, and others were worried about economics, finance, the reaction of the British, an Arab attack.

Ben-Gurion went ahead, in the teeth of all opposition, and proclaimed the state — and we know what happened. If it may be said that the act of one man can change the course of history — a moot point — then Ben-Gurion did so in proclaiming the State of Israel. Had he done nothing more, he secured his immortality on that 15th day of May, 1948.

The late Dr. Azriel Carlebach once remarked that to meet Ben-Gurion in the flesh and shake hands with him gives you the sensation of meeting Judas Maccabeus. This was no exaggeration; it is still no exaggeration. But we must be forgiven for not remembering it every time we see Ben-Gurion. And we are entitled to criticize some of his actions and policies since 1938. As long as he is immersed in the squalid business of politics, he cannot expect us not to. Nor does he, in fact. He if often compared to Winston Churchill, a comparison that holds good at many points, from standing alone to having the vision of the shape of things to come. Churchill was, nevertheless, removed from office by the will of the electorate when they considered him unsuitable for postwar tasks. The same fate might well have befallen Ben-Gurion, and it would not have detracted from his greatness. But Israel is still at war, and Ben-Gurion still watches over its security. What is more, he has come to symbolize it. To be in a state of war and yet feel secure· is a unique position, unique even more for a small state, and Ben-Gurion is the architect of this security.

Here is another paradox: Ben-Gurion, the hyper-active politician, the restless statesman, the shrewd party tactician, the master of political maneuver, has become a father figure in Israel and among world Jewry, the symbol of the assurance that Israel is here to stay for another thousands years and more. It takes moral courage to criticize or decry a symbol. Denigration of a symbol is tantamount to sacrilege, and those who suggest doing away with a symbol incur the anger of the multitude and are taunted with the dark accusation of courting moral collapse and physical disaster. Without going into the merits of the various conflicts, we must grant it to Ben-Gurion's detractors that they too have moral courage.

It is said that Ben-Gurion's devoted lieutenants, able and effective men like Shimon Peres and Teddy Kolek, are often severely, loudly, and even unfairly criticized because the critics really mean Ben-Gurion but cannot find it in their hearts to attack him. So they make his aides their targets. These aides act as lightning conductors for Ben-Gurion. But it is, of course, to the ordinary citizen, the so-called man-in-the-street, that symbols appeal most. When Ben-Gurion came back as prime minister in 1955 and took over from Sharett, a Tel Avivian — an ordinary Jew without any sophistication whatsoever — said to me:

"You know, I am very fond of Sharett. I admire him as a man, a scholar, and a statesman, but I sleep sounder since Ben-Gurion is back." The condition for sleeping well is, of course, one's own state of mind, and not necessarily an objective appraisal of a situation.

Two more instances where moral courage of the highest order were brought into play by Ben-Gurion are the Suez campaign and the Eichmann trial. Perhaps the Eichmann trial required even more moral courage than the Suez campaign. After all, the Jews had defeated the Arabs once before; there were sound strategic reasons for going into action; and that state of war is not of Jewish making. It needed moral courage, though, to take a decision instead of drifting, to overcome internal opposition, and to ignore warnings from outside. But there was no precedent for such action in the Eichmann case. And there was no telling how the Jews, inside and outside Israel, would react to the drama.

To go back a little in time, the "Altalena" case, too, required moral courage. A ship manned by Jews was fired at by other Jews. This may have been the most heartbreaking decision in Ben-Gurion's whole career. As to whether it was the right one, the historian of the future, with all the facts before him, will have to pass judgment. And there are bound to be different opinions even then. But this does not affect the quality of the decision in terms of moral courage.

Next to moral courage, the most significant characteristic of Ben-Gurion is best described in the time-honored Hebrew formula of *Ahavat Yisroel*. It may be translated as love of one's fellow-Jews, or love of the Jewish people as a whole, but neither has the flavor of the Hebrew. In Hebrew it also implies love of those in distress, which is a higher quality than mere brotherly love. But, of course, it does not exclude an abiding hostility towards individuals in powerful positions who are in the way, or are competing in any sense. Human nature is rather complex, and the character of great men is much more complex than that of ordinary mortals.

I came face to face with this quality in Ben-Gurion many years ago. It so happened that I was one of the first group of war correspondents to enter Dachau upon its liberation. Apart from the need to share this stunning experience with other Jews, I had many letters and messages from survivors, some of them old friends, and all of them Jewish martyrs for whom one wanted to do something in one's humble way. So I secured a lift to London in a military airplane — a uniform went a long way in those days — and went to the office of the Jewish Agency Executive. They told me Ben-Gurion, then the chairman in Jerusalem, was visiting London. He was told where I came from, and I saw him within five minutes.

He let me talk for a long time. I told him what I had seen and what the survivors had asked me to convey. He was shaken to the core, and kept on saying: "We cannot revive the dead, but we shall have to care for the survivors, and make them forget and start new lives." Then again: "Is a new life possible after so much suffering? Perhaps it is. Human beings are very resilient, and Jews are even more resilient than most." These casual remarks, more to himself than to me — I was not interviewing, an interview would have been utterly out of place — later on appeared as elements in a great oration where he said: "We shall bring them home on our backs."

He asked about the reaction of the Germans. I said they were groveling now and denying they had been Nazis. To this he remarked: "A people that can swing from murderous bullying to abject groveling are not a nice people. Shall we ever be able to forgive them? Are there any Grmans who are different from the Nazis?" Those were rhetorical questions. He was asking himself, not me. His meeting with Dr. Adenauer some fourteen years later may have been, in a way, his answer to this question.

Before I left, he said. "We have a few *Aliyah* certificates. It is so painful not to be able to take the survivors home immediately. But I shall send twenty-five, all I have at the moment, to show that we have not forgotten them."

Ben-Gurion had assessed the psychology of the survivors accurately, though he had not seen any at the time — May, 1945. When I told them in Germany about those twenty-five certificates, for 2,800 survivors who all wanted to go at once, they said: "We know he had no more certificates. It is good to know we are remembered." A committee of the survivors soon allocated the certificates. In Israel, I still meet some of those who were chosen to go. Only recently one of them, a Chief Inspector of Taxes, reminded me: "You know, of course, I was one of the twenty-five *Olim* with Ben-Gurion's first certificates. I would have gotten here just the same eventually, happy, overworked, and underpaid, but Ben-Gurion with his gesture took all the 2,800 home, in a spiritual sense, and thus preserved our self-esteem."

There is that element of *Ahavat Yisroel* in Ben-Gurion's attitude to the oriental communities in Israel. And also in his attitude
to non-Zionists and his inclination to forgive former opponents,
even bitter opponents, of Zionism and all its works. To suggest,
as some Zionist leaders did, that all this is done to spite the
Zionists, is both unfair to Ben-Gurion and unworthy of the people
who advance such theories. God knows, Ben-Gurion is a formidable controversialist and a stubborn opponent, and is often in-
capable of forgiving those who have crossed him. But such failings, however irritating and frustrating to others, should not tempt
anyone to retaliate by accusing the greatest Jewish leader of our
generation, the architect of the Jewish State, of so mean and
squalid a maneuver as hobnobbing with non-Zionists to spite their
local Zionist opponents. Even if it were true, we should all deny
it for our own sakes. But it isn't really. *Ahavat Yisroel* can exist
side by side in one person with abiding hostility towards individuals who are Jews or Israelis, as indicated above.

However, this exasperating streak in Ben-Gurion's character,
his inability at times to be magnanimous, his almost devilish determination to eliminate adversaries, especially those of his own
party (and this is not surprising: it happens often in politics),
came to the fore in the Lavon Affair. Whatever the rights and
wrongs of the issue itself, Ben-Gurion must have known that his
furious drive against Lavon, an almost maniacal campaign, was
not in the interests of Israel. But he could not help it, obviously.

Like so many men who had no time or opportunity to delve
into the vast treasures of human knowledge in their younger
days, Ben-Gurion is forever fascinated with these treasures, inclined to be uncritical when he encounters new ideas and theories,
and eager to share his newly acquired intellectual experiences
with other people. A good example of this well-known condition
was his address at Brandeis University where he shared with his
audience his new experience of Eastern philosophy. He was
genuinely fascinated by it and desirous of imparting his fascination and edification. There was nothing new or startling in what
he said, nothing original except a few asides, incidental to the
theme, but it had the freshness of the convert to a new idea. In
this sense it was rather engaging. He displayed the same eagerness
when he paid his two visits to Oxford and was browsing among
the books of a famous bookseller, climbing the ladders and
bending to the low shelves, feasting his eyes like a traveler entering Aladdin's cave. This is not the case of an elderly man re-
reading books he had encountered in his student days, or reading

books he knew were there but had had no time to read. It is that of a man with a receptive mind and a thirst for knowledge and intellectual experience trying to make up for lost time and to recover lost ground. At seventy-six he is still one of the busiest men in the world. But he cannot afford now to keep the books on the shelves until he will have time to read them.

While Ben-Gurion no doubt enjoys the intellectual exercises as such, he cannot help relating it to his daily needs as a practicing statesman. The uses of the Bible to Ben-Gurion — and this does not mean that he does not enjoy the Bible for its own sake — are threefold: as a pattern for strategy; as a source of inspiration; as a warning. Strategy is conditioned by terrain, at least in orthodox warfare, and the pattern of the biblical wars was repeated in 1948 and 1956 to a remarkable degree. It is probably not by accident that a great archeologist like *Yigael Yadin* was the successful Chief of Staff of the Israeli Defense Forces at the most critical time in the state's history, and that his successors in this office have all been students of the Bible and history, Jewish and general.

Ben-Gurion, never far from detailed planning, makes the Bible his textbook. The greatness of Israel in the days of King Solomon. the grandeur of the prophetic vision, the ethics that are enshrined in the Book, must have their lasting appeal to a man of Ben-Gurion's stamp. Finally, the warning, both explicit and implicit — the secession of the Ten Tribes, the fate of Samaria, the strains and conflicts in Jerusalem before the destruction of the First Temple, and even more so before the destruction of the Second Temple (for that one must go to later sources, but Ben-Gurion does not stop at the Bible; he is not a modern Karaite) — is always on Ben-Gurion's lips. He obviously lives with it. Which is a very good thing for Israel and all Jews. That he forgets it sometimes in the stress of humdrum party politics, and thus causes dangerous situations, merely goes to show once more that he is human. That ephemeral conflicts are blown up by him to large but unreal proportions is, again, natural. Our sages have known it long ago: *"Kol Hagadol Mechavero Yitzro Gadol Heimenu"* (in a free translation: "He who is greater than his fellow-men also possesses a greater impulse for wrongdoing").

The belittling of the total achievements of the Golah is, of course, not seriously meant. The immersion in ancient glory; the drive to bring to Israel as many Jews from the Golah as possible; the conviction, shared by many, that no Jewish position in the Golah is secure — all combine to produce those Ben-Gurionisms about the gap between the First and Third Commonwealth (from David to David, the wags say). He often, though, gives himself away by quoting the Bible in the Ashkenazi pronunciation, which is Golah through and through. It is also relevant that his knowledge of the Bible is much more profound than his knowledge of the Mishnah, Talmud, Gaonic and Rabbinic literature and lore. A man tends to take illustrations from the texts he knows best. The trouble is that many of us, actively encouraged by his uncritical admirers, are sometimes inclined to take seriously everything Ben-Gurion says. To retain a sense of proportion, we must always remember that Ben-Gurion usually states his case in extreme terms, and then subjects his statements to numerous revisions, sometimes as the result of criticism and sometimes of his own accord.

The best example is perhaps the continuous dialogue between the Prime Minister and American Zionists. On the American side the participants in the dialogue change: it is sometimes a Hadassah spokesman (or is it spokeswoman?), sometimes a B'nai B'rith leader, sometimes a veteran Zionist, sometimes even a theoretical exponent of "Diasporaism." On the other side it is always Ben-Gurion, still going strong, battling against all comers, and more often than not, having the better of the argument.

The Ben-Gurion logic is faultless, as logic goes: The adage that the Almighty did the Jews a great favor by spreading them among the nations of the world has lost its validity. It was true while the survival of the Jewish people depended on the salvation of one part, even as other parts were persecuted and exterminated. Now the survival of the Jews depends on the survival of Israel. Survival can thus be made certain by the active participation in Israel of Diaspora Jews from the West, by their personal commitment through Aliyah. Israel needs their experience, their knowledge, their know-how. It needs their monetary contribution, too, but this is secondary. If they refuse to come, they fail in their duty.

Thus Ben-Gurion in so many words. And he has on his side the whole Jewish tradition: The *Mitzvah* of living in the Holy Land is greater than all the others put together. But life is not governed by sheer logic, and human nature does not always respond to a logical argument in terms of deducing the consequences. This Ben-Gurion knows. In fact, he has made peace with the idea that a mass *Aliyah* from the West is not likely in the near future. He cannot, however, forgive the Zionists for not living up to their beliefs, and he refuses to accept the idea that Zionism retains special tasks in the Diaspora. This rejection is allied to the purely

administrative inconvenience of having the Jewish Agency in
Jerusalem as a body with special status. He accepted it reluctantly, and is not enthusiastic in living it.

So he goes on preaching that Diaspora Zionism has served its
purpose and should dissolve into a general Jewish organization
to help Israel, foster Hebrew education, and promote *Aliyah.*

Teaching children Hebrew is next-best to *Aliyah,* according to
the Ben-Gurion doctrine. But this is done by all Jews nowadays.
Israel itself, by being there, is the best propaganda for Hebrew. At
the same time, Diaspora Zionism refuses to meet Ben-Gurion even
half-way, and continues as before. Here too is a vested interest,
over and above the genuine and sincere argument of principle.
Public bodies have a tendency to perpetuate themselves.

The flaw in Ben-Gurion's position is not his logic but his in-
sistence that our generation must tie up all loose ends, arrive at
a final formula for Israel-Diaspora relations, and implement it at
once. He does not want to leave anything to time. The idea that
time itself is a great teacher and a great healer does not seem to
occur to him. This is understandable. Men like Ben-Gurion do
not like to leave things which they consider vital undone, for the
next generation to finish. They hate delegating authority; they feel
they can do it better. Ben-Gurion does not want to share the fate
of his namesake, who was not vouchsafed to build the Temple.
He knows, of course, that a people is not born in a day, and
he quotes the prophet on this. But he does not like it. He would
dearly want to leave things tidy.

There is always evident in Ben-Gurion's character that subconscious wish to defy the laws of nature, to redeem the spirit
from the shackles of the flesh. Here is a giant of a man, with his
intellectual powers undiminished at seventy-five while the body
sometimes feels its age. I chanced to see him once in London,
about a year ago, as he was just arising from his afternoon sleep,
refreshed and alert. He said: "A nap in the afternoon still washes
out my tiredness." It was the assertion of the will to make the
body obey the spirit. Hence Yoga, the art of concentration and
control which enables one, apparently, to detach the spirit from
the flesh and defy nature. Ben-Gurion's method is Yoga as
adapted to the Western mind and adjusted in the light of modern
medicine.

That famous cartoon of Ben-Gurion standing on his head and
reading a morning paper that is held upside down by a secretary,
is the most telling description of this phase in Ben-Gurion's quest

for spiritual and physical self-improvement on behalf of the Jewish people.

The attraction of Plato for a man like Ben-Gurion is obvious. He is constantly in search of perfection in the art of government. The Platonic idea of the three lives of a man — the philosopher in quest of wisdom, the man of action driven by his ambition, and the man of appetite for life, almost fits Ben-Gurion. Only on the third score does he not live up to the Platonic description, and never has done so. His private life is governed by his public life. There seems to be no particular desire to sample the good things of life in any aspect, unless reading be termed indulgence. Then there is the Platonic precept for constitution-making. This, according to Plato, should be done by the Academy. Which is all right with Ben-Gurion, provided he is at the head of it. And being an amateur philosopher, he considers himself fully qualified.

In his polemics Ben-Gurion does not seem to be able to separate the argument from the man. There is a personal dislike of opponents. Not only does he never admit for one moment that they might be right, he does not even seem to admit that what they say may seem to them to be right. Nor would he grant them the right to say with Plato's disciple who disagreed with the Master, "I love Plato but I love the truth even more." On reflection, perhaps. After a time, possibly. But not while the argument is still raging.

With all this Ben-Gurion does not consider himself a perfect human being. His quest for self-improvement is constant and sincere. Hence the lure of Buddhism. Perhaps also the fact that the goal of Buddhism is knowledge, not morality. To learn and rule is an ideal state for a man like him.

The flirtation with Buddhism was of some years standing before that famous journey to Burma. That Ben-Gurion should go to Burma was only natural, in view of the friendly relations between the two countries. That he should want to see everything is also natural. The East has its lure for all of us. That he should want to see Buddhism in action was to be expected. And who would not, given such an opportunity? But the study of Buddhism was given as one of the objectives of the journey. This was strange for an active politician. A prime minister in office must, at least formally, have politics as the main purpose of any journey, unless it is a private occasion. He can't have his incense and burn it, as it were. But who says he can't? Apparently B.G. can.

Of course, it is difficult to say how well up in Buddhist exercises he is now, or whether a week of instruction and contemplation added much to what he did know already. On the other hand, it was preposterous to suggest that the head of the Government of the Jewish State should not indulge in the exercises of Buddhism, which is a way of life and not merely a religion.

For a man in search of new knowledge and anxious for self-improvement, there is the obvious attraction in Buddhism: right views, right intentions, right speech, right action, right concentration. These are excellent precepts for a prime minister. An inner harmony and peace, to the point of seeming lazy. Not that Hillel did not teach us some of this; not that you can't find similar injunctions for behavior in the wisdom of our own sages. But here it is concentrated in an ethos, while our sages gave it as marginal comment and free advice. And it comes from a strange and mysterious region way across half the world.

Perhaps no one but Ben-Gurion could have got away with such a gigantic escapade. The abiding affection with which he is regarded makes people smile indulgently and forgive him many things. It is all summed up in one Hebrew word, *Hazaken,* very much like "the Old Man" in English, implying veneration, affection, license to be different, but least of all old age itself.

Ben-Gurion's public life and private life are one and the same. His private life is so uncomplicated that it merges into his public life without embarrassment. Mrs. Paula Ben-Gurion is, however, not just the prime minister's wife or the Old Man's faithful companion; she is a striking personality in her own right. She combines the self-effacing devotion to duty of the nurse (which she once was) with the exhibitionism of the actress (which she never was). She is wise, but incautious in comment. She is voluble, and yet never betrays a secret, though she knows many. She is humorous, and yet takes herself seriously. Whether Ben-Gurion is no hero to her — is any husband to his wife? — one cannot say, but if he is not, she hides it well. Altogether, Paula Ben-Gurion too is a fascinating personality.

David Ben-Gurion has said: "Let us not be too proud; let us not get drunk with our victory . . . We have not accomplished all this alone . . . three generations of settlers preceded us here . . . And let us remember the Jews of the Diaspora who had suffered as we never did and had had a faith no less strong than the one that had inspired our soldiers in the war of independence . . ."

This should be taken as reflecting the attitude of the true Ben-Gurion — by all of us, and by him as well.

Noah Barou

The Price of Involvement

Like the Poets, politicians may also be divided into those who are involved and those who are detached. It is primarily a matter of temperament, although there are other elements in it, too.

Involvement and detachment should not be confused with identification and non-identification. A detached politician also identifies himself with the people he represents and speaks for, but he guards his private spiritual and physical existence against intrusion by his public duties and responsibilities. To speak of keeping job and hobby apart is merely to describe a mode of life, as does the ivory tower simile. Detachment goes much deeper than that. It means a detachment of the soul, which can be achieved even by a person leading a busy life and spending all his waking hours in contact with people. Involvement is, of course, the reverse of detachment. An involved politician not only acts but also feels deeply; his inner sanctum is constantly invaded by his anxieties; he is possessed by his concerns even when he has physical privacy.

The prophets are the archetypes of involved public figures. "For the sake of Zion I shall not hold my peace!" is the classical outcry of the involved man. This problem is particularly well defined in the story of the minor prophet Jonah. In contrast with other prophets, Jonah was obviously a detached character. He shirked the task God had assigned to him, and he was told off in no uncertain terms. For God loves the people who are involved and has no use for those who are detached.

Noah Barou belonged to the category of the involved. Indeed, he was involvement personified. He came from a background where detachment was unknown and an ideal demanded everything, leaving no room for physical relaxation of mental respite. Much more important, Barou's temperament was that of an involved man. He belonged to the order of Those Who Care. Like all Those Who Care, Barou lived his life in terms of his ideal. This left no time for frills, small pleasures, or diversions.

He lacked, too, that cynical streak which serves many a leader as a safety valve when tension becomes unbearable.

Noah Barou was born in Poltava, the Ukraine, in 1889. His was a Jewish middle-class background outside the Pale of Settlement, one where many of the children were given a secular education combined with Jewish knowledge, which home and surroundings amply supplied. Because of the *numerus clausus,* few of these children were lucky enough to get into schools of higher learning. Yet some of the able ones found their way, and Noah Barou belonged to this category.

Barou went from Russia to Heidelberg. On arrival there, he left his luggage at the railway station and marched off to the famous university to see a professor whose permission he sought to join a particular seminar. When the professor inquired on what date this new and somewhat unusual visitor proposed to join the seminar, Barou replied: "Right now, Herr Professor. Please give me your permission, tell me how to get there, and I shall proceed to the seminar from here."

Barou did not participate in university life. There was no time for that. After some years in Germany, he arrived in England with a doctorate in economics. His specialty was the Co-operative Movement. It was not by accident that he came to England when he moved westward from Germany. The Co-operative movement was born in England and spread from there all over the world. It started as the Equitable Pioneers' Society in a small Lancashire town, Rochdale, in 1844, and grew into a mighty organization, embracing a producers' wing, known as the Wholesale Co-operative Society; a distributive wing, known as the Co-operative Society, with hundreds of stores all over the British Isles; a bank; an insurance company; and a political party, the Co-operative Party, affiliated with the British Labor Party (to which only a small fraction of the many millions of co-operative members belong). It is easy to see why a man like Barou, in quest of further knowledge of the workings and impact of the Co-operative Movement, turned up in England. It was very much like a mythographer going to Greece or a student of the Bible going to the Holy Land.

In England Barou found his métier. He soon joined the Fabian Society. This society was organized in 1883 and named after Fabius Cunctator, the Roman general famous for his effective delaying tactics, because the founders believed in the necessity of long deliberation before taking action. Bernard Shaw, Beatrice and Sidney Webb, and Graham Wallace were

Juliet Pannett.

among its early members. Today the Fabian Society is a body for research and study serving the Left. It publishes surveys, papers, and books on social, political, and economic problems, and enjoys a high reputation for its work. Indeed, it is now a British institution.

The Fabian Society was made to order for a man like Barou, eager to learn and to teach, anxious to make his contribution towards the improvement of the human condition. In 1932 he published his *Co-operative Banking;* in 1936, *Co-operative Insurance;* in 1944, *World Co-operation;* in 1947, *British Trade Unions.* There were also papers, pamphlets, and books on Russian co-operation, a subject on which he was considered one of the world's greatest experts, as well as on Russia generally.

But Barou could not remain a purely' theoretical economist and political scientist. It would have been totally out of character. He was soon a member of the committee of the Fabian Society and a member of the International Institute for Co-operative Studies. Along with these activities in general society, he was extensively involved in Jewish affairs. He served as a member of the Board of Deputies of British Jews, chairman of the European Executive of the World Jewish Congress and member of its World Executive, and in a leading position in the Trades Advisory Council, an organization of Jewish industrialists and businessmen for combating discrimination in trade and industry as well as for supervising trade standards.

With all this, Barou somehow found time to work for a living. He was an economic consultant of a very high order. He also had a profound knowledge of the workings of international finance and the stock market in various countries. This he put to good use, making productive investments for himself as well as for his clients. It made him financially independent, which was essential for a man like him, given to speaking his mind fearlessly.

In Heidelberg, Barou acquired knowledge but refused to learn method; he developed his own method, one which suited him perfectly. He had a tiny fountain pen, a remarkable gadget which became a Barou hallmark, and he was forever feverishly scribbling with it in a small notebook, crowding the pages with assertive Russian characters. Everything went into it: notes for speeches: reminders to himself to attend to various chores; names of people with exclamation marks after them, indicating that they were in need of help or advice; material for a book or an article; statistics and facts; ideas and scraps of ideas to be looked into at some future date. It was a kind of treasure house, and the tiny pen was a faithful servant that constantly added to the treasures of its master.

Barou's Russian was superb, but his English was indifferent. When he came to England, he was already too much immersed in other activities to be able to settle down in a seminar for English, as he had settled down in the economics seminar at Heidelberg. His English grammar was made passable — barely — by his common sense, but his accent remained thick. Only Barou could get away with it, not only among British Jews but also among English intellectuals. Because he cared so much, he always spoke with his whole being. Thus he could rivet the attention of his listeners to the flow of ideas and the construction of an argument, completely diverting their attention from the fauly mechanics of his speech.

Like many young Jews of his generation in Russia, he had early been attracted to the political Left, becoming active in Socialist circles at the age of fifteen. When he died in London at sixty-seven, he had behind him fifty-two years of public service.

Just what was the ideal to which Barou devoted all his adult life, more than half a century of brainwork of a very high order? Barou once summarized it for me in one of his rare moments of idleness, while he was awaiting a telephone call from abroad. "The object is to improve the lot of our fellow human beings," he said.

This, indeed, sums up Barou, the man and the political figure. He had chosen his ground at the age of fifteen — socialism, in its widest and noblest meaning. But his common sense and his knowledge of history drove him to the conclusion that the lot of his fellow-Jews could not be improved without special treatment, that Jews did not always fit into the general scheme of things. Hence his activity in the Poale Zion Left, the ideological precursor of the present-day Mapam, and his later devotion to the World Jewish Congress. Barou's Zionism and his dedicated work for Israel in the last years of his life had nothing of the messianic mood in them; they were the result of contemplation which led to inevitable conclusions.

Barou was a man designed for large matters. He could not confine himself to local politics or communal affairs, even those of such a metropolis as London. He habitually reflected on humanity as a whole; he always thought of Jews in global terms.

Soon after the liberation of Europe, he threw himself into work on behalf of the Jewish D.P.'s (Displaced Persons). He became their guide, mentor, and trusted friend. It was to his London home that they telephoned whenever there was trouble. He also spent much of his time in the camps, especially Belsen, which was in the British Zone of occupied Germany.

Perhaps the dedication to Barou in the Belsen Book best sums up his contribution to the rehabilitation of the D.P.'s:

> Noah Barou was one of the first among the free Jews who came to see us after liberaiton. He gave us not only his knowledge and his wisdom and his experience and his political acumen, but most important, his heart. He shared our sorrows and our joys as one of us; he identified himself with us completely. He never wearied of listening to our troubles and his devotion lasted out until the last Jew left the camp. . . .

At that time he began to ponder over the possibilities of repairing at least some of the ravages the Nazi era had wrought upon Jewish life. His approach was that of an economist; he deliberately suppressed his emotions so as to be able to calculate coolly both the damage and the chances of some restoration. I remember the time he told me: "Germany will soon be prosperous again: I know the Germans. Having killed the victims, now the Germans keep the loot. Are they to murder and inherit and get away with it? Individual survivors should get their property, or its equivalent, back; the Jewish people should be the heir to Jewish communal property; Israel should be compensated for all she did to harbor the Nazi victims; she is the real successor to the martyrs."

I remarked that the idea sounded just and fair and reasonable, but would Jews accept it? Would Israel accept it? Would not the Jews say that they did not want German money? Was there any chance of any kind of dealings with Germany in our generation? To which Barou replied: "What you say has occurred to me many times. I am having sleepless nights over it. But Israel needs the reparations for her survival, or at least for her economic progress. And Israel is the most important consideration. If Israel fails, God forbid, it will be the end of the Jews as a people, and our enemies will then have scored their final victory. This must never happen. We must overcome our revulsion and see that some reparations are paid to us."

This was early in 1946. Barou was the originator of the idea of German reparations. It took some time for the idea to mature in

Barou's own mind. Discussions with Dr. Goldmann and other
intimates took more time. The Government of Israel had to
persuade the Israelis to accept the idea. Meanwhile, Barou became a one-man task force to probe the views of the other side,
to prepare for the first meeting, to act as go-between in the
three-cornered approaches between Israel, the Diaspora Jews,
and Germany. It was a delicate and exhausting task, exhausting
physically as well as emotionally. Barou persisted in it right
down to the signing of the Luxembourg Agreement. He was a
director of the Claims Conference from its inception until the
day of his death, but there were so many directors — some without title or claim to such office — that the originator of the
idea never received due credit.

Long talks with Barou were only possible on occasions when
circumstances kept him from activity. Such opportunities were
provided by the long drives in my car when we used to go together to the conferences of the British Labor Party, which
always take place at holiday resorts. Barou would settle down
in the car and close his eyes for a brief nap while I got through
the heavy London traffic; he would wake up when the road
ahead was clear and I was free to chat with him. On one such
occasion he looked out over the Kent autumn landscape and
said it reminded him of a Levitan painting which he owned. He
was a great admirer of Levitan and had a number of his can-
vases. He explained to me that one could relax looking at man-
made art, and that gazing at nature was not absolutely necessary
for relaxation. I suspected that this was merely a rationaliza-
tion, an excuse for a restlessness which gave him no quarter,
left him no time to go off into the countryside and forget everything for a few days.

On another occasion, Barou remarked that tolerance must
be cultivated at all costs, because without it one would despair
of democracy and succumb to fascist ideas. The efficiency of
authoritarianism had no allure for him. "Efficiency is not everything," he said. And then: "For heaven's sake, don't apply
this maxim to your driving!" This was Barou the conversationalist
delivering one of his asides. When I remarked that I would
not, because I had given Sophie (his wife) my word to look
after him and bring him back safely to Hampstead, he said: "Ah,
if only I could get myself to listen to Sophie I would feel much
better . . ." But he could not. He was a dedicated man who
burned himself out in living up to his principles.

Juliet Pannett

Ernest Boris Chain

The Penicillin Drama

THERE IS an unmistakable resemblance to Nietzsche in the appearance of Ernest Boris Chain, the Noble laureate, who isolated penicillin, determined its structure, and established its curative properties. The thick moustache; the assertive head with its rich, vital, dark hair, a little more disciplined than those of the archetype; the powerful shoulders, and the general stance put Chain among the Nietzsche types of men.

But here the similarity ends. The great biochemist, who is now investigating the action of insulin and the interrelation between carbohydrate and amino acid metabolism in brain and nervous tissue, could not possibly entertain any ideas about supermen and destiny. If Nietzsche and Chain had been contemporaries, and Chain had had the opportunity to have a go at Nietzsche, he might have been tempted, I fancy, to divert Nietzsche's character and abilities to more useful channels, with the help of a compound that adjusts the brain without damaging it.

It strikes me that if Chain were to be elevated to the peerage — which would not matter one way or another, but is not an impossible contingency — he might choose for his motto "Dust Thou Art and to Dust Returnest," not in the pessimistic sense — for the interval can be usefully and excitingly employed — but in the sense that man is, in the final analysis, but a biochemical formula.

Chain's career is typical of those of a number of Russian Jews who made their way from Russia to Germany and thence to the Anglo-Saxon world, where they achieved fame and left their mark. A select few of them have so profoundly influenced our physical existence and spiritual outlook as to attain immortality. Chain is very likely to be classified among those few, when the time for a full evaluation of his contribution comes. But he is still in his early middle age, at a stage of thinking and planning ahead rather than summing up.

Ernest Mikhailovich Chain, to use the good old Russian designation (which Chain himself sometimes uses, partly out of nostalgia for his Russian-Jewish home and partly because he is amused by its strange sound to English ears), was born in Berlin in 1906. His family came from Mogilev, Russia. His father, a chemist and factory-owner, was a friend of Chaim Weizmann, whom Ernest knew from early childhood.

Chain graduated from Berlin University in chemistry and physiology and came to England in 1933 as a refugee from Nazi persecution. He worked at Cambridge and after two years moved to Oxford. There he remained until 1948. At Oxford, Chain worked on snake venoms, on the action of lysozyme, on tumor metabolism, and other problems. At the end of a study in the biochemical mechanism of the action of lysozyme, Chain suggested to Sir Howard Florey the undertaking of a systematic study of antibacterial substances produced by micro-organisms. "The idea was, in fact, simple," Chain says, "because the bacteria-killing properties of the earth have been known since biblical times. They already knew in the days of Moses that a body buried in the ground is no longer infectious, even if it is the body of a human being who died of a contagious disease."

Florey agreed to Chain's suggestion and, on his part, proposed that lysozyme should be the particular object of the study. Chain then dug up and read some two hundred papers in this field, which helped him to clarify his own ideas and stimulated new avenues of thought. "You must read a lot of papers before you embark on your own line of inquiry," Chain says, "and never despise anything that was written earlier, however remote or antiquated. There may always be the germ of an idea somewhere."

Among those two hundred papers was one written by Sir Alexander Fleming in 1929. Fleming was a keen observer in the laboratory but not an original scientific thinker. Chain decided to work on the substance observed by Fleming because some chemical work on it had already been done. This was, in fact, penicillin. It proved to be an extremely unstable substance, which was the reason Chain became interested in it. He first thought it was an enzyme acting in the cells of the organism, but he soon found out that it was not an enzyme but a low molecular substance unstable both in acid and alkaline solutions.

At this point Chain and his collaborators were a little disappointed that penicillin was not an enzyme. They thought it would turn out, after purification, to be a member of one of the many groups of known antiseptics, such as phenols. But when they discovered that on injection the substance was not toxic, despite its antibacterial power, "the situation became very interesting," in Chain's own immortal understatement. There was no team at the beginning of this work. The team was gradually assembled as the need arose, the elucidation of the chemical structure took place, and the clinical trials started. This investigation led to the discovery of the curative properties of penicillin and ushered in the era of antibiotics.

Between 1942 and 1946 Chain wrote several memoranda, two of them to the Medical Research Council, in which he suggested pilot-plant facilities be made available for work of this kind. But his suggestion was not accepted. The argument was that work of this kind was not "academic" enough. When Chain persisted, some bigwigs became audibly annoyed at the audacity of a "Polish Jew" telling them what was what.

There was also an earlier memorandum by Chain to the Rockefeller Foundation (in 1938) in which he suggested taking up the study of antibiotics produced by microorganisms and mentioned other substances, in addition to penicillin, which have antibacterial properties. He proposed that those be studied after penicillin. This was six years before the streptomycin discovery by Waksman. There is no doubt that had Chain been given the pilot-plant he had asked for, he and his collaborators would have extracted at least some of the numerous antibiotics of curative importance. It was as if they were looking at the things, knew the things were there, but lacked the means of extracting them.

Fortunately, Chain ignored his critics and did not resign. He is not the type of a self-appointed martyr on the altar of science — you know, the type who struggles on against all odds and continues to work on his idea at his wife's kitchen sink while the children go hungry. He is a proud man and a proud Jew, sure of himself and eager to get on with the job without waiting until all reactionaries, fools, and bigots are finally convinced.

In 1948, the Italians invited Chain to come to Rome and work at the Instituto Superiore di Sanita, and he accepted the invitation. He went to Rome because he was offered pilot-plant facilities there of the type he had envisaged all along. In Rome the discovery of 6 amino-penicillanic acid led to the discovery of numerous new penicillins, some with very "interesting" properties. This achievement was only made possible by the use of pilot-plant fermentation techniques, which Chain had in Rome but was denied at Oxford.

While working in Italy, Professor Chain acted as adviser to a team of research workers at the Beecham Laboratories in England. There they discovered that the main part of the penicillin molecule (the 6 amino-penicillanic acid) could be made by biosynthesis and afterwards modified by chemical means. Numerous new antibiotics can thus be made, including a type of penicillin which is acid-stable and can be taken by mouth, and which attacks staphylococci resistant to normal penicillin. We may be on the eve of a revolution in the field of antibiotics.

The guidance Chain was able to give the Beecham team was, at least in part, the result of his work in Rome. It was there that he found a full outlet for his genius. In England Chain shared the Nobel Prize with Fleming and Florey; in Rome he was relieved of frustration and permitted to do things his own way, which is so essential to a man who knows his own mind and is sure of the aims which he pursues.

The wider public in England hardly knew about Chain's part in the penicillin drama. Fleming was almost canonized. He is the hero of a biography by André Maurois, the biographer of Disraeli and other outstanding names in the *English Dictionary of National Biography*. Only the experts know what Chain's contribution was. In 1949 he was elected a Fellow of the Royal Society. He is also an honorary member of several academies and learned societies in other countries, and holds many honors and degrees of various universities, including the Sorbonne, as well as high decorations of the French and Italian governments.

But Chain is not bitter about England — successful men are usually inclined to forgive. There is only a slight hint of contempt when he talks about the reactions at Oxford and Whitehall to his early ideas. Nor does he identify a few fatheads with England. "I love this country," he remarked recently while talking to science correspondents in London. So he came back from Italy when the University of London offered him the chair of biochemistry at the Imperial College of Science — but he did not do so unconditionally. The Isaac Wolfson Foundation made available 350,000 pounds for the building and equipment of laboratories for biochemistry and chemical microbiology, where teaching and research is being organized the way Chain wants it. In fact, the project at the Imperial College embodies the same type of pilot-plant facilities which Chain built up at Rome. He is very glad that after all these years it has finally materialized in England. All the scientific and technical resources of the Imperial College will be available to co-operate in the project. There are problems which must be farmed out to organic chemists ("I was one myself but degenerated into biochemistry," Chain says), chemical engineers, and plant physiologists. And they are all there, at the Imperial College, right next door.

Chain's ability to make every complicated problem look surprisingly simple, which is the hallmark of great men, together with his spontaneous gaiety and wit, make him a good teacher as well as a good companion. His inquiries into the mysteries of nature are inspired by a compassion for his fellow men. Fundamental research is the starting point and prime condition for success, but the practical results are cure of disease, relief of pain and anxiety, and a more wholesome life all around.

Chain himself has a flair for the good things of life. In London he always stays at the Dorchester, a hotel both luxurious and expensive. But this flair is tempered by a desire to make the good things of life available to others too, rather than an attitude of "I'm All Right, Jack."

Chain bears his Jewishness lightly. No conflicts, no apologies, no attempts to separate the two levels of existence. He is a lifelong Zionist, naturally. Home background, a knowledge of men and affairs outside the limited field of science, logic, and sentiment all combine to make his Zionism organic. "I am devoted to Israel," he will tell you, "and captivated both by its magic and its achievements." In his own field he is a constant guide and mentor to the Weizmann Institute at Rehovot, always available to them for advice and consultation, as a matter of course.

Mrs. Chain, a biochemist in her own right, is one of the Beloffs, a sister of Professor Max Beloff and of Norah Beloff, writer and foreign correspondent. The Chains have a boy of six, Benjamin, and twins of three — Daniel and Judith. Chain's face lights up when he speaks of the children. Perhaps unusual for a man of his preoccupation, he is not an absent-minded parent, but a diligent and utterly devoted father.

Ernest Boris Chain will be remembered in history as the scientist who converted penicillin from a scientific curiosity into a powerful therapeutic agent. He will take his place alongside Ehrlich, Lister and Pasteur.

Isaac Deutscher

Juliet Pannett.

Isaac Deutscher

The Original Sovietologist

SOVIETOLOGY is a comparatively new science. In fact, the name has not yet established itself, though it is being increasingly used. But whatever the designation, the science is there, and its practitioners enjoy a special position and are given great attention—for obvious reasons. Sovietology is the study of the Soviet Union, and this includes, of course, Soviet politics, the Communist Party, Soviet economy, Soviet literature, and Soviet art, as well as Russian history from its very beginning. No sovietologist worthy of the name would start from 1917. For a proper understanding of Soviet Russia one must go back to the early beginnings at Kiev in the days of Rurik.

Genuine and reliable sovietologists are very rare in the West; there are none in Russia, naturally. It is possible for an American or an Englishman to become a good sovietologist, as it is possible for an American or an Englishman to become a good sinologist. In fact, some of the great English sinologists have spent their lives at Oxford or Cambridge, and I know at least one who has never been to China. But an East European background and an instinctive understanding of the Russian mind is a great help to a sovietologist; personal acquaintance with Stalin, Lenin, Trotsky, and Khrushchev is less important.

Isaac Deutscher, a Galician Jew who is now a British citizen, is among the world's greatest sovietologists. I consider him the greatest of them all. In 1949, Deutscher published his *Stalin, a Political Biography,* and at once established himself in the front rank of Soviet experts. This was followed in 1950 by *The Soviet Trade Unions.* In 1953 appeared Deutscher's *Russia — What Next?* and *Russia After Stalin. Russia in Transition* was issued in 1957. In 1959 came the first two parts of the Trotsky triology, *The Prophet Armed* and *The Prophet Unarmed.* The next year produced *The Great Contest — Russia and the West.* Parallel with these major works, there was a stream of essays, articles, broadcasts, lectures, and book reviews by way of marginal com-

ment, amplification, or postscript to the major works. Deutscher
writes in English; his books are translated in almost every modern
language. They are also available on both sides of the Atlantic
in paperback editions and various other forms, cheaper and more
widely distributed than the august books of his original publishers,
the Oxford University Press.

Bertrand Russell has said of Deutscher: "Mr. Deutscher is to
my mind the most intellectually satisfying of the many writers on
Soviet Russia." John Dewey said very much the same in discuss-
ing Deutscher's *Stalin.*

And now I can begin from the beginning. Isaac Deutscher was
born in Chrzanow, near Cracow, in 1907. He comes of a family
of printers, publishers, and scholars. His grandfather had a print-
ing shop in Cracow, where he published prayer books, tracts, and
sundry religious-scholarly writings, all of which are known by
the general name of *Sforim.* Some of these he wrote himself. But
while remaining a deeply pious man, he did not shun secular
scholarship. The family had a tradition of dissent. Isaac's father
lived in Chrzanow, where Isaac spent his childhood. He was a
businessman and a journalist in his spare time, the local correspondent of *Hatzefirah,* the Hebrew daily founded by Chaim Selig
Slonimsky and made famous all over Eastern Europe by Nahum
Sokolow, who edited it for many years. Deutscher *Père* must have
been a fine writer to be published by Sokolow, a very fastidious
editor.

Yet the father remained a deeply religious man, and he
brought up Isaac in the same spirit. Isaac attended a *Yeshiva*
and was known as an *Ilui* (a youthful genius, in free translation)
before his *Bar Mitzvah.* To seek secular education was a break
with tradition in his family. Still wearing his ringlets and Hassidic
garb, he passed the entrance examination at the local Polish high
school and soon mastered Polish to perfection. Later on he made
use of the extra-mural facilities of the University of Cracow. He
had his teachers and mentors in those days, but he is essentially
a self-educated man, with all the strengths and weaknesses of this
type of scholar. It should be noted here, in parenthesis, that such
a course is not suitable for children less gifted and intellectually
less tenacious than Isaac Deutscher was.

Still wearing his traditional garb and retaining the air of a
Hassidic youth, and with a *Semicha* (a rabbi's certificate, issued
by an authority on the strength of a candidate's sheer knowledge)
in his pocket, Isaac Deutscher was already writing—and publish-
ing—Hebrew and Polish poetry. He read his Polish poems at

student gatherings, and he frequented literary circles. He translated Bialik, Tschernichovsky, Shlonsky, Uri Zvi Greenberg, and other Hebrew poets into Polish. Zionism was the natural next step; Deutscher became a contributor to the Cracow Polish-Jewish daily, *Novy Dziennik,* a Zionist newspaper.

The breakout from the Jewish milieu came in 1925, when Isaac Deutscher joined the Polish Communist Party to look there for remedies for social ills, which he could not find elsewhere. He soon made his way to the top by sheer brainpower, and became an editor of Polish Communist publications, a position he retained until 1932. This was an activity both clandestine and unremunerative. For a living Deutscher, who by then had moved to Warsaw (Galicia became part of Poland after the First World War), worked as a proofreader on the *Nasz Przeglad,* a polish-Jewish daily in Warsaw, to which he was also an occasional contributor. He was not, of course, a run-of-the-mill proofreader, and this was recognized by Tlomacka Thirteen, the Jewish writers' and journalists' center in Warsaw. He was hobnobbing with the great of the center, the literary lions, on equal terms, and he even lectured to large audiences. It was a dual existence, but one not rare in those days. To live a second life underground was the lot of many in a country without political freedom.

In 1931 Deutscher went to Russia, by a roundabout route, as a member of a delegation of Polish Communists. He met many of the leaders of the Soviet Union, but not Stalin. Him he saw only from a distance. It would have made no difference, of course, if the author of the classic on Stalin had shaken hands with his future subject. Gibbon and Momsen had never seen a Roman Emperor; nor has André Maurois met Disraeli.

In 1932 Isaac Deutscher was expelled from the Polish Communist Party as an anti-Stalinist, one of the first of the genus. There were other points too, on which Deutscher disagreed with his party. This was the dissenter again. In between, Deutscher served in the Polish Army. He is not the type that makes good soldiers, but he managed, somehow.

In his fierce arguments with his comrades in the Polish Communist Party, Deutscher is on record as having forseen Hitler's invasion of Russia. He was described as a "spreader of alarm and despondency." (This should not be taken to mean that Deutscher's forecasts and prognostications invariably turn out to be correct. He does not claim it himself). From orthodox Polish Communism Deutscher veered towards Trotskyism, but found no satisfaction

among the Trotskyites and soon left Poland altogether. He came
to London.

I used to meet Deutscher in London in the early days of the
war. He was already a detached character, without political affilia-
tion and without ideological shackles, applying his inquiring mind
to the ways of the world. We would sometimes walk from the
Ministry of Information through the quiet squares of Bloomsbury
—unusually and strangely quiet between air raids—and Deutscher
would hold forth in his slow, pontificating voice, and in a very
fine Yiddish, about the war and its aftermath. In those days we
smoked the cheapest cigarettes on the market, and Deuscher
could not always afford even those, but he seemed to be more
anxious to make his impact than to make a living.

I remember coming across him a few days after the German
invasion of Russia. *"Ir Zet,"* he said in Yiddish, which can be
well rendered in English as "I told you so," but without the sting
of recrimination (it would not have been applicable in my case,
anyhow).

But to go back to the early days of the war, the old adage,
"You can't keep a good man down," once more proved true.
Deutscher became a contributor to important English journals,
such as the *Economist,* the *Observer,* the *Times* and the *Manchester Guardian.* English is no problem to an *Ilui.* It may not be
possible for him to acquire the accent of a native, but he can
surely take acquiring the art of writing good English in his stride.
From penning articles for English quality journals Deutscher
progressed, after the war, to the writing of books. He was for a
time the "Peregrine" of the *Observer;* he produced many fine
pieces of journalism; but he had things to say that could only be
developed in books.

But why a biography of Stalin? I mean, why this form for saying
what he had to say about Russia, its place in the world and its
relations with the West? Not long ago Deutscher told me why: He
was most at home in economics and philosophy; he had the background, the knowledge, and—perhaps most important—the feel
for a study of Russia after the Revolution. He believed, too, that
the time was ripe for such a study. He considered himself, probably rightly, the best man to embark upon it.

But could an abstract way of writing, an analysis of ideas and
their impact upon practical politics, an inquiry into the history
and development of Russian Communism and its destiny, appeal
to the Anglo-Saxon mind? If English was to be the medium, then
the form would have to appeal to this type of mind. Thus, he

decided on a political biography. Here the poet in Deutscher came to the rescue. With data assembled, facts marshaled, and developments traced and analyzed, the instinct of a poet helped to produce a classic of biography. Stalin is not merely a peg for Deutscher's thesis; he is the subject of a study, not only in power, but also in the vagaries of the human mind in general, and in the psychology of a Georgian cleric who rose to rule all the Soviet People in particular. Stalin had more power than any of the Czars ever had, and because he represented an idea, too, he had infinitely more impact upon the world outside Russia.

Deutscher was right. His *Stalin* soon became a best-seller-cum-reference book, and the author had arrived at last. Such an arrival compensates for old frustrations and releases new energies. Trotsky was his next subject, even as Trotskyism followed Stalinism in Deutscher's own development. This necessitated a study of the Trotsky archives at Harvard. Deutscher proceeded to the source. He knew what to look for and, of course, how to read and interpret the material.

The first two volumes appeared in quick succession — Deutscher's industry always matches his mental capacity — but the story could not yet be finished. One part of the Trotsky archives was not to be opened before 1980, at the injunction of Trotsky himself in his testament. The only person able to waive this injunction was Trotsky's widow. But she did not at the time take kindly to Deutscher as an author and sovietologist. And no wonder. Some critics had described Deutscher as a "Stalinist." They did not know about his quarrel with the Polish Communist Party; they based their opinion on Deutscher's thesis that Stalin did a lot of good, though at a very high price — a view he repeated recently in a B.B.C. interview. There were also some devoted Stalinists who considered Deutscher an "anti-Stalin" writer. For did he not say that Stalin's work would endure only after a thorough cleansing of Stalin's methods, and thereby cast aspersions on Stalin the man? Neither of those two schools of critics was right, of course. But the label of "pro-Stalinism," at any rate, stuck for a time.

However, Madame Trotskaya, an intelligent and perceptive woman, changed her mind after reading Deutscher instead of his critics. The two met, and she gave him permission to read the sealed archives. Harvard had no objection. And so the third and last volume of the trilogy will be based on these papers, never before read by an outsider. I have seen the manuscript of this third volume resting in a drawer in Deutscher's study — a bulky folio straining to be released, as it were. It promises to be an exciting book.

Today Deutscher leads the life of a busy English writer, working from a retreat in the countryside. He has three other books in preparation, one of them on Jewish problems. His home, a large and comfortable house with beautiful grounds, is at Wokingham, Berkshire. This is known as an "exclusive" district, a few miles from the famous race course of Ascot and quite near Windsor Great Park. Deutscher himself blends into this background rather well, and there is little trace in him of the Yeshiva of Chrzanow. He is now bald and bespectacled, sports a small goatee (shades of Trotsky!), dresses in fine tweeds, drives a fast car, and even walks the dog. He tends to expound rather than talk or chat, but a natural courtesy and a sense of humor save him from being ponderous.

At a time when the West is so anxiously trying to understand Soviet Russia and puzzle out Russian actions, a man of Deutscher's achievements, knowledge, and reputation tends to be looked up to as a sage. I suspect that Isaac Deutscher enjoys this role, though he will tell you that callers and correspondents take up a great deal of precious time.

Deutscher's Yiddish is rather halting these days, though when he visited Israel he did lecture in that language so as to be properly understood. His Hebrew, which he knew so well in his younger days, is today practically non-existent, which is surprising. A language may get rusty with a person who does not use it, but can a man with a good memory and a flare for languages forget a tongue in which he once wrote poetry? Yet it is true in Deutscher's case. It is as if he has pulled his deep Jewish roots out deliberately, by an act of will. For there is surely room for another language in his formidable intellectual apparatus. He is now a true internationalist in his outlook, a British citizen by adoption, and an Englishman in his habits and mode of life. He has not so much cut himself off from his former friends as added very many new ones. His only son, Martin Charles, a boy of twelve, to whom he is very devoted, is being brought up in this atmosphere.

Deutscher has been an anti-Zionist since the time when he joined the Polish Communist Party. Today he "recognizes" the existence of Israel in very much the same way that Professor Morozov "recognized" the Russian Revolution — simply because it is there. It is there for him also in a more personal sense — his sister is a founder-member of the Israeli *Kubbutz* of *Mishmar*

Haemek. But he is on record as saying that "Israel arrived a hundred years too late; now the nation-state is on the way out, notwithstanding the emergence of all those new states in Asia and Africa." He said this publicly recently; he did not hesitate to imply it several years ago in Israel; he reiterated it the other day in a conversation with me. At the same time, he admits he was wrong in opposing Zionism so fiercely between the wars, since Palestine, and later on Israel, did save Jews from extermination in the European holocaust.

The detached objectivity which is Deutscher's hallmark these days loses its completeness, and with that its power to convince, when he speaks of Israel. There is somewhere in him a vestige of the avowed anti-Zionist. Israel can do no right in his eyes: her economy is untenable; her treatment of the Arabs in the country is suspicious. On Israeli economics Deutscher is theoretically perhaps nearer the mark than on other aspects, but this should cause no alarm. His approach is that of the pure economist, one of those good economists whose advice Herzl, Weizmann, and in our days Ben Gurion had to ignore. Otherwise there would have been no Jewish State. It is simply that Deutscher does not feel the mystique of Zionism, which he might have done had he not forgotten his Hebrew so completely. Nor does he grasp the sense of partnership between Diaspora Jews and Israel, as yet undefined and unformulated, but nevertheless working all the time in a thousand ways.

Still, he may be classified not as an opponent of Israel but as a somewhat biased critic. Since he is not a Ben-Gurion fan, he may yet write Ben-Gurion's biography. Ben-Gurion received him once, and they had a conversation. Which is more than Stalin did.

It is my wont to conclude a piece with the nicest item I can think of. This is why I have left Tamara Deutscher for the last. Tamara is a clever, intelligent, and charming woman, of the kind whose good looks stem from personality rather than conventional beauty. She is her husband's secretary, research assistant, critic, and inspiration. It is Tamara who shapes the masses of recorded and jotted-down notes into usable background material. Deutscher is fond of recounting that when he first met her, she told him sternly that he was late. Soon afterwards, she typed a letter for him and told him to delete a passage, which he promptly did. "And this," he says, "is still the refrain." But he seems to enjoy it enormously.

Nahum Goldmann

The Art of Persuasion

NO MAN in the long history of the Diaspora has ever been entrusted with so many exalted public offices, nor has anyone ever represented in his person so many facets of Jewish life, as does Dr. Nahum Goldmann. The mantles of both Chaim Weizmann and Stephen S. Wise have fallen upon his shoulders: he is the president of the Jewish Agency and the World Zionist Organization, as well as of the World Jewish Congress. He is also the president of the Conference for Material Claims against Germany.

I have advisedly avoided using the term "power" in trying to delineate Goldmann's position in Jewish life. Jewish life is not coherent and organized enough in the Diaspora to give any man, however exalted his position or great his influence, real power of decision on behalf of a majority which binds all and can be put into effect. The nearest thing to it is a right to speak for Diaspora Jewry and a personal influence which can sway decisions when action is needed. And this Goldmann has, most of the time.

Nahum Goldmann was born in Wisniewo, White Russia, on July 10, 1894. His parents took him to Germany when he was six years old, but his home background remained intensely Jewish. He spoke and read Hebrew — taught to him by his father, a Hebrew teacher — long before he had the full use of any European language. He went to high school in Frankfort. A brilliant career at the universities of Marburg, Heidelberg, and Berlin followed. The "Dr." in front of his name stands for a Ph.D.

Goldmann began his post-university life as a scholar, co-editing (with Jacob Klatzkin) an encyclopedia and writing essays and pamphlets of a political and philosophical nature. But it was not long before his flair for oratory and his interest in public service asserted themselves and took him away from his books, never to return.

Juliet Pannett.

His rise in German Zionism was smooth, and he soon branched out into the world Zionist movement. In 1935 Goldmann was elected for the first time to the Zionist Executive. Thereafter until the outbreak of World War II he represented the Jewish Agency for Palestine, as it was then called, in Geneva, the seat of the League of Nations, which was the ultimate, if not effective, authority over Palestine. The Leagues Mandate Commission was the receiving agency for reports on the British administration of the mandated territory. This legal situation may not have had much practical value at the time, but when Ernest Bevin, years later, found himself in an impasse, he tossed the mandate back into the lap of the League's successor. The resolution of the United Nations provided the legal title for the Jewish State, though the world being what it was — and still is — the armed forces of the Jews of Palestine had to carve the state out and secure its existence.

It was in those Geneva years that Goldmann came to be known as Zionism's ambassador-at-large and made his contribution to the political struggle that eventually resulted in the State of Israel. Almost simultaneously, he branched out into Diaspora politics, as distinct from Zionist activity. In 1936, he joined Stephen S . Wise and others in founding the World Jewish Congress. Since then his activity has continued to follow two parallel lines — Zionism and Diaspora Jewish affairs. Each of these fronts presented a struggle — the one a struggle for the right of the Jews as a people to have their own national home, the other a struggle for the elementary rights of Diaspora Jews in many countries.

After Hitler came to power, Goldmann left Germany for good and resided in Switzerland, where the Republic of Honduras granted him "courtesy citizenship." In 1940 he settled in the United States, and today he is an American citizen, though hardly an American Jew.

Goldmann's stature as a leader among Diaspora Jewry reached its peak after the war. The Jewish State came into being and thus became the sole master of its own foreign policy. Goldmann remained essentially a Zionist leader, and a leader of Diaspora Jewry. But the interests of these three converged at the point of negotiati n with Germany over material claims, as they did and still do at other points less sensitive and less important.

Goldmann was the natural Jewish negotiator with the Germans. Position, experience, and talent all pointed to his person. The preliminary approach, the spadework, was done by the late Dr.

Noah Barou, who originated the reparations idea in the early days after the holocaust. Barou never received full credit for it until after his death, when Goldmann gave him his due in a valedictory speech in London. The negotiating body, the Conference of Jewish Organizations, was Goldmann's creation. He brought the twenty-two Jewish organizations together and became the president of the Conference, as well as its liaison man with the Government of Israel, before and after the Israelis appeared at Luxembourg, where the agreement with Germany was signed.

At the very outset, the Claims Conference, as it is now known, made it quite clear that "crimes of the nature and magnitude perpetrated by Nazi Germany against Jews cannot be expiated by any measure of material reparations." But there was the enormous material damage caused to Jews, and it was a matter of historical justice that this damage should be made good on both the collective and the individual levels, and that the funds should be used to rebuild Jewish institutions in the Diaspora, where possible, as well as to shore up Israel's economy, groaning as it was under the strain of absorbing the Jewish homeless after the war. Eretz Israel had, of course, also been the haven of most of those who made their escape from the Nazis between 1933 and the beginning of the war.

The reparations agreement was signed at Luxembourg on September 10, 1952, and came into force on March 27, 1953. It committed Germany to pay Israel $822,000,000 in commodities and services over a period of twelve to fourteen years. Of this sum, $107,000,000 was earmarked for the Claims Conference, which has been using the proceeds for Diaspora needs. The Claims Conference thus became not only the receiving agency but also the distributing agency for the funds, a task which was — and still is — as delicate as it is complicated. Goldmann remains the unchallenged head of the Claims Conference, and its life and soul.

There was bitter resistance to the agreement with Germany both in Israel and in the Diaspora. Goldmann had the vision of the future before him when he persisted against all opposition; he grasped the need and formulated the reasons for accepting the German reparations without loss of national pride. I heard him say once that, as a Jew, he would have been ashamed if there were no resistance to this agreement with Germany. He understood the feelings of those who went so far as to threaten his safety during his frequent visits to the Jewish State. (In fact, at one stage the Israel authorities had to provide him with a security guard.) In time, the opponents of the agreement calmed down and the bitterness abated. This was a victory for Goldmann on a painful issue and in a great debate among the Jewish people.

During the war, the British used to have huge posters at all railroad stations and air terminals (the Americans copied this fine exhortation later) asking: "Is Your Journey Really Necessary?" Goldmann is one of the most widely traveled men in the world — he spends a considerable part of his life in the air or in hotels — but there is no doubt that his journeys *are* necessary. Since Diaspora statesmanship is still a matter of persuasion, a kind of glorified *Shtadlanuth* (interceding — in rough translation), Goldmann's presence is required wherever Jewish affairs are discussed on a high level with non-Jews. Even in internal discussions among Jews, Goldmann can seldom leave matters to his aides. He is the best, and often the only, persuader who can influence Jewish public and private opinion and make Goldmann-esque ideas acceptable to most Diaspora Jews. This ability to make friends and influence people (Goldmann could have written his own version of Dale Carnegie's famous book) is doubly important to a statesman in Goldmann's position. For he represents no tangible power. He has neither Weizmann's *Yishuv* nor Ben-Gurion's authority, vested in him by the Knesseth and backed by a large number of Isael's citizens, to fall back on.

Actually, Goldmann represents an assortment of Jewish citizens of some eighty countries, who give him their spare-time allegiance, as it were. Before he can proceed further, he must persuade those with whom he deals that all these people, as Jews, represent a coherent force, and that their representative is worth listening to; or, alternatively, that moral issues count in this turbulent and chaotic world of ours. He must also persuade the Jews of the Diaspora that they can defend their rights and their positions only by being an organized and united body — which is perhaps the more difficult of the two tasks, and certainly the more heartbreaking. It is always heartbreaking to have to state and state again and state once more something that should be obvious. But some people are too shortsighted to grasp it, or too selfish to accept it.

Again, the affluent society, in which most Diaspora Jews have their full share, makes it extremely difficult, and sometimes impossible, for Goldmann to rouse Jews to meet challenges and dangers that look ahead. Goldmann himself formulated this problem in his own inimitable way: "We know how to survive in conditions of adversity; we must learn how to survive in conditions of ease."

It is difficult enough to fight on two fronts; Goldmann fights on three: there is also the continuous dialogue with Ben-Gurion. They disagree over the role of post-State Zionism; they do not see eye to eye on the ultimate destiny of the *Golah,* as Ben-Gurion prefers to call the Diaspora—and the different terminology is but the outer symptom of a different philosophy. To many Israelis Goldmann remains an outsider, a Zionist who did not settle in the Jewish State. Even to some of those who oppose Ben-Gurion's policies and methods Goldmann remains a visitor, presidency of the Jewish Agency and all the rest notwithstanding. When he intervened in the last Israel general election in support of the Liberal Party, there were voices even among his own friends and admirers in Israel saying that he could only do harm by intervening from the sidelines, as it were. Opponents made much of this somewhat unnatural situation. That Goldmann brilliantly defeated them in argument and established his case for participating, is another matter. He could not allay the vague feeling among Israelis that there was something not quite in order in such a procedure, though they all admitted that, Israel being a free country, Goldmann should be given a hearing. That was the sort of expression one heard time and again — "given a hearing." Applied to the president of the Jewish Agency and the World Zionist Organization, it is almost an insult, though prompted not by ill will but by the very human reaction of those who are sweating it out, not to mention spilling their blood, against those who enjoy the fleshpots of the *Golah.* Goldmann often becomes the target of this resentment.

This sort of existence as a statesman would have daunted a less resilient man long ago. His inner strength, stemming from great intellectual power combined with immense self-confidence, bordering on the arrogant, (the two often go together), brings him through these vicissitudes unscathed.

Goldmann's roots are in Eastern Europe and in Jewish culture. On top of this is a layer of German culture, absorbed and digested. Even today Goldmann knows well — really well — only Hebrew and German. His Yiddish is slightly Germanized in the use of terminology, though natural in the use of idiom; his English is fluent but poor in idiom and is sometimes badly constructed syntax-wise; his French is quite good. His accent and inflection remain Yiddish when he speaks English or French. When he had to learn those two languages, he was already too busy to devote any substantial time to them and too self-confident to bother very much. Strangely enough, he remains a magnificent orator in all the languages he speaks, one of the greatest among Jews, and a great orator by any yardstick. Some of his speeches remain memorable.

Every man experiences some sort of inner revolution in his younger days. Goldmann's made him a founder-member of the Radical Zionists and one of the leaders of that group which revolted against Weizmann's slow progress as well as his policy of accommodation at all costs with the British Mandatory power in London and Palestine.

For a man of Goldmann's temperament — he is essentially a negotiator not a revolutionary — this must have been a violet upheaval. Before long, however, he entered also into general Jewish politics, a field in which the defense of human rights by argument is the main task.

Goldmann's métier is the defense of rights by argument; he would be completely out of his element if he had to take up arms, actual weapons, against those who fail to react to logical and humanitarian reasoning. This, in the final analysis, is why Goldmann chose to remain in the Diaspora and argue, when others of his generation of leaders went to Eretz Israel and argued only in their spare time, doing other things as well towards the upbuilding of the Jewish State.

And therein lies the tragedy of Goldmann. He himself may not have time to stop and think of it, except perhaps on a sleepless night, but it is nonetheless a tragedy. A man of his pride and mental equipment, condemned to *Shtadlanuth,* however polished, without the opportunity of normal statesmanship; a Zionist of his ability, standing, and devotion, condemned to stay in the Diaspora and lead Jews from the air, as it were, while lesser people are members of the Knesseth, ministers, and party leaders in the Jewish State; an orator of his persuasiveness, condemned to deliver his speeches on public platforms in hired halls, while smaller fry make their speeches in the Parliament of Israel and have them recorded for posterity in the Official Record.

This tragedy is reflected in one aspect of the Ben-Gurion-Goldmann dialogue, the question as to whether Zionists should have a share in the shaping of the destiny of Israel while remaining in their own countries.

Not that Goldmann argues from an individual point of view. Of course not. But a person's mind is conditioned by his own experience. Nor can he escape from his subconscious. Goldmann pleads for the perpetuation of Zionism as a force in Jewry and as a partner with Israel, at least in matters of destiny, if not in the daily chores of foreign politics and internal affairs. He advocates the supremacy of the Jewish people over the Jewish State. To him the Jewish State is simply the major instrument for the preservation of the Jewish people. Ben-Gurion sees the state as the consummation of Zionism and the only instrument for the survival of Jewry. This, logically, leaves no room for a specific movement in the Diaspora, now or in the future. It means the winding up of Zionism as soon as may be convenient. To Ben-Gurion, all Jews who do not come to Israel are junior partners, "helpers," and there is no special position for Zionists in this partnership.

There is an inclination to appease in Goldmann's character. His mind may have been conditioned that way through his constant efforts to co-operate with various and diverse Diaspora Jewish bodies. To be sure, appeasing the weaker is a virtue not a vice; and so Goldmann's hankering in public for peace with the Arabs is not necessarily a sign of weakness or lack of character and stamina. He tries to see whether there is room for compromise with the Arabs now, in our days. But he does not understand the Arabs as well as he does the Europeans. Goldmann does not seem to realize that talk of peace with the Arabs, and restatement of the geopolitical truth that Israel happens to be in the Middle East, is regarded by the Arabs as a sign of weakness. They will make peace when they are convinced that Israel is there to stay for another thousand years, with or without peace.

In his dealings with the Germans, Goldmann is much more in his element; he is the good negotiator talking to people whom he understands well, the diplomat trying to achieve his ends by negotiation, the Diaspora statesman for the first time truly speaking on behalf of all Diaspora Jews.

Dr. Goldmann has no challengers for the leadership of the Zionist movement or of the Claims Conference. But the first is a faded glory and the second a temporary office. There is still the World Jewish Congress, but the leader of this body does not always speak for all Jews. A lesser personality than Goldmann would have had even less opportunity to appear as the spokesman of all Diaspora Jews by virtue of leading the World Jewish Congress; even Goldmann is often let down on this score. It is an on-off process, like a plunger controlling one of those twinkling neon signs.

Goldmann's place in Jewish history is assured, of course. The attempts to capture his private personality, as distinct from his public image, are, therefore, both understandable and excusable. He seems not to have mastered the modern media of mass communication, such as broadcasting and television, and few people know the man well from personal contacts. But his is an infinitely interesting personality: he is an expert in the art of living, a connoisseur of the good things of life, without being ostentatious or offensive about it, a possessor of an astonishing brain, which switches easily and gracefully from theme to theme, from situation to situation, from interview to interview, with the smoothness of a good engine, a past master of witty table talk, an expert on detection, a lover of the arts. He has a wife and two sons, but Goldmann's private life is kept strictly apart from his public life.

Goldmann, the man and the statesman, is one of those people whose strength is in their *presence* — this despite a not very imposing physical appearance. He is short and square, with ordinary features, mousy hair, and a gait betraying the lack of sporting activity in his younger days and of exercise now. He is a lazy man who can afford to be lazy because his grasp is so quick and his energy can be summoned at will. He is reported to be writing his autobiography, but autobiographies of egocentric men — and Goldmann is one — are hardly ever a reliable source of objective data, though usually very good reading as well as a tempting field of inquiry for the psychologist.

Dr. Goldmann, never really an American, has now moved his base from New York to Geneva. Nobody actually lives in Geneva, unless he is a local Swiss, but it is a geographically and politically convenient base of operations for the president of the World Jewish Congress at the present juncture in Jewish politics. As he was in the process of moving to Geneva, Dr. Goldmann publicly announced that he would settle in Jerusalem in the fall of 1963.

In the context of the Ben-Gurion—Goldmann dialogue, this is an important move for Goldmann. The argument as to whether we still need Zionists in the Diaspora or whether Jewish friends of Israel would be a more effective instrument to help the Jewish State will continue, probably into the next generation. But Goldmann will now be arguing from a stronger personal position.

It will be too late for him to occupy an effective and prominent place in the Government of Israel. For that he should have come in 1948. But he will be speaking for the Zionists from Zion. And when the final balance will be drawn, the Jerusalem phase will undoubtedly be taken into account.

Robert Henriques

The Conversion of an Anti-Zionist

IN 1876 THE Victorian English novelist George Eliot (pen-name of Mary Ann Evans) published *Daniel Derona*. It is both a very readable novel and a strong intellectual plea against anti-Jewish prejudice. The real-life prototype of the novel's hero was Colonel Alfred Goldsmid, one of the few *Hovevei Zion* ("Lovers of Zion") in England, who in his later years became an ardent supporter of Herzl. Of this Colonel Goldsmid it used to be said that he was "the perfect example of an English officer and gentleman."

Colonel Robert Henriques is an Anglo-Jew in the tradition of that nineteenth-century figure. Nowadays Henriques describes himself as an "elderly Englishman." This is a charming understatement. Henriques is not simply a retired colonel; he is also a famous novelist, a distinguished journalist, a popular broadcaster, and a gentleman-farmer in the best English tradition.

Robert David Quixano Henriques was born in 1905, the scion of an old Anglo-Jewish family of whom it can be truly said that they came to England with Menasseh Ben Israel. He is a Sephardi, of course, like all the early Jewish settlers in England three centuries ago.

Henriques was educated at Rugby, a famous English public (i.e., private) school, and New College, Oxford. Somewhat unusually for a Jew and a man of letters, he served in the army as a regular officer until 1945; during the Second World War he was a commando in the field and, later, head of the Planning Section at Combined Operations Headquarters. Among his several decorations are the Silver Star and the Bronze Star of the United States.

In 1938 Henriques published his firstbook, *Death by Moonlight*. His novel, *No Arms, No Armour,* came out the next year and won the British Empire Prize and an international prize for literature. *Captain Smith and Company* (in America, *The Voice of the Trumpet*) appeared in 1943, and *The Journey Home* (in

America, *Home Fires Burning*) in 1944. *Through the Valley* followed, and won the James Tait Black Memorial Prize. Next came *The Cotswolds, A Stranger Here,* and *Red over Green. A Hundred Hours to Suez,* a totally different kind of book, appeared in 1957. This one belongs to Henriques' post-conversion period, and I shall return to it a little later. Henriques latest book (1960) is *Marcus Samuel, First Viscount Bearsted,* a biography of the founder of Shell, who was the author's grandfather-in-law.

A Gloucestershire farmer, a hunter, and a member of the Cavalry Club, Robert Henriques never, however, became an assimilated Jew in the ordinary sense. He was—until recently—one of those Anglo-Jews who remain faithful to the religion of their fathers but live a full English life and have no desire to be active as Jews. True, he was for a time a member of the Board of Deputies of British Jews, but then the Board consists of representatives of synagogues, which makes it a religious body.

Henriques told about his conversion in a remarkable and moving speech when he appeared for the first time at a Zionist gathering. It was a public confession by a man of high moral courage. A famous writer laid his soul bare before the whole world, permitted us a glimpse into the depths of his being, and told us things which most people are afraid to tell even themselves.

"I was against a Jewish state," Henriques related, "until it was created. Once it came into being, there was no more room for argument. However, I did not think that the State was any concern of mine; I had towards it an attitude of friendly neutrality.

"And then something happened to me. Suddenly, on sheer impulse, I sat down and wrote a letter to the Ambassador of Israel. I had a cordial reply, and the Ambassador invited me to talk with him and gave me a very good lunch. He did not call me to account for my indifference in the past."

Henriques went to Israel in 1956, met Ben-Gurion and Dayan, who was then Chief of Staff, lectured to the Staff College, and fell in love with the Jewish State. He asked Ben-Gurion what he could do to be of service to Israel, and Ben-Gurion replied, characteristically: "Send your children to see the country."

When the Sinai campaign started, Henriques went back. He wanted to help. After all, he was an officer with great experience both in fighting and in the planning of battles. But he came too late — the swift campaign was already over when he landed at Lod. As a result of his trip, however, we have that fascinating book, *A Hundred Hours to Suez,* which is not only an appraisal

Robert Newigin
1962

Juliet Pannett.

by a great military expert but also a classical narrative of war by a
fine writer. Henriques devotes a lot of space to the human factor
in this campaign. He is one of the few outside Israel to have
grasped the paradox of men devoted to peace doing battle with
consummate skill. Only lovers of peace — when they discover
that there is no other way out — are capable of fighting with such
fury and mastery.

It did not take Henriques long to absorb the spirit of the Israel
Army. Only a Jew could have done it so well and so fully in such
a short time. And so Henriques has given us a great book, and
dedicated it "to the People and Army of Israel."

I return to his confession. On that memorable occasion, he told
us that he still believed about open, militant anti-Semitism that "it
cannot happen here;" but that if he were wrong and it did
happen, it would be the duty of British Jews to stay in England
and fight it out, together with all decent Englsihmen. Yet there
was a mystical force which tied him to that country and he has
built himself a house in Galilee now. He could not explain it,
and it was all the stronger for that, since it did not depend on
argument.

He said: "I once had a keg of Israeli wine. When I decided
to dispense it into bottles, an expert told me not to do it just
then, as it was the time of the blossoming of the vine in Israel
and the wine in my keg was in a restless, disturbed and agitated
state. If the power of the vine in blossom can affect the wine in
my keg two thousand miles away, why should not the power of
Israel affect a Jew in some mysterious way at the same distance?"

This is the only explanation Henriques is able to offer for his
conversion, his newly-found attachment to Israel. The voice of
generations, a mysterious force which demands identification.

This metaphysical kind of Zionism has led Henriques to understand so well the force that is hidden in the State of Israel. It
made it easy for him, a complete stranger, to feel at home in Israel
on the day of his arrival.

"Before Hitler," he says, "I used to whisper that I was Jewish;
after Hitler I used to say it in a rather loud voice; in Israel I
discovered for the first time that I was saying it in a simple, normal
way, as somebody stating the obvious."

The conversion is complete. Henriques says: "I can hear a
voice calling from inside my being: 'I am a Jew'. . . . 'I am a
Jew'. . . . 'I am a Jew'. . . . I am not trying to run away from it.
Of course I am a Jew. Hence my special and peculiar attachment

to Israel. This force is in me, though I cannot define it in terms of logic and common sense."

Henriques cannot explain *why* he has "come home," but he tells eloquently *how*. And in this respect he is the spokesman for many once-estranged Jews who have "come back" since the Jewish State came into being. He puts their feelings into words for them — which it is the duty and the privilege of a writer to do.

Leslie Hore-Belisha

A Mystery Resolved

FOR TWENTY YEARS after Leslie Hore-Belisha resigned as Secretary of State for War in 1940, the incident remained shrouded in mystery. His resignation was both unexpected and bewildering. For he was one of the most successful war ministers in British history. Neville Chamberlain, who was then Prime Minister, described him as the best War Minister since Haldane. Indeed, it was Hore-Belisha who had reshaped the British Army in preparation for the war against Germany — a great achievement, carried out in the teeth of opposition from generals and politicians alike. Why then did he resign?

Hore-Belisha himself did not offer any clues at the time, nor did the Prime Minister. And so for two decades the mystery continued to exercise journalists, politicians, and historians, as well as the general public. (Here it should be noted that the British have a positive passion for pursuing political mysteries. They are still probing to discover whether Roger Casement, the Irish Leader, was guilty of sexual misconduct, and whether Lord Derby liked or disliked Lord Curzon. Why, Robert Graves is still trying to find out who poisoned the Emperor Claudius!)

Then in 1960 appeared R. J. Minney's *The Private Papers of Hore-Belisha*. Minney had access to all the Hore-Belisha diaries but chose to confine himself to Hore-Belisha's term of office as War Minister. At last the mystery of the sudden resignation was resolved.

But first some background. Leslie Hore-Belisha was a Sephardi Jew, born in London, in 1893. His father died when he was five months old, and his mother remarried a Mr. Hore — hence the hyphenated surname. He went to Clifton College and Oxford, where he was president of the Union (the Students' Society), entered politics as a liberal, and became a Liberal-National (or Liberal-Conservative) at the time of the split in the Liberal Party, in 1935. His parliamentary rise was meteoric. Before long he became Minister of Transport, a term of office whose lasting

Juliet Pannett

monument is the "Belisha Beacon" which marks pedestrian crossings all over Britain. Two years before the Second World War broke out, Hore-Belisha moved up to the War Office, where he soon made his mark by introducing better terms of service in the Army, especially for privates (enlisted men) and non-commissioned officers, and by reorganizing the War Office itself, until then a stronghold of the type of officer known as Colonel Blimp. The Army reforms established Hore-Belisha as one of the trailblazers of the welfare state.

Hore-Belisha's political success was the result of a clever and charming personality, a considerable intellect, a flair for public relations (at a time when that now pervasive art was almost unknown in Britain), skill in oratory, and a genuine interest in the common man. He was popular with the man-in-the-street but was disliked by most of the generals and many of the members of that Conservative stronghold, the Carlton Club. He was not "one of the chaps" — and was a Jew to boot. Moreover, he took advice from Liddell-Hart, the famous military scientist, instead of heeding the "brass hats" at the War Office.

Hore-Belisha managed to overcome the opposition of the generals when he rebuilt the Army into a citizens' force, but then he made another decisive move, one which proved his undoing. On a visit to France, he discovered that the "impregnable" Maginot Line was too short — it did not reach to the North Sea. Upon returning to London, he demanded drastic action to close the gap before it was too late. But General Ironside, Chief of the Imperial General Staff, and Lord Gort, Commander in Chief of the British Expeditionary Force, both of whom had been installed by Hore-Belisha in the teeth of determined opposition from many quarters, combined against their political chief behind his back. Together they betrayed the confidence he had placed in them, let him down in a moment of crisis, and insisted that he must go or else there would be "prejudice" in the Army (the language used by Chamberlain). Chamberlain had hitherto backed Hore-Belisha, but now, when the pressure of the generals became too great, he asked his War Minister to resign.

More light on the Hore-Belisha mystery is shed in a new biography of Neville Chamberlain by Iain Macleod, one of the ablest Conservative leaders, until recently Secretary of State for the Colonies and now chairman of the Conservative Party and Leader of the House of Commons.

Macleod recalls that Chamberlain had held Hore-Belisha in high regard and sent him to the War Office against the advice of highly placed Tories. He wrote about Hore-Belisha in a private letter: "My new Secretary of State (for War) is doing what I put him there for and has already stirred the old dry bones until they fairly rattle."

When some ministers tried to remove Hore-Belisha from office in 1938, Chamberlain backed him. But in 1940 Chamberlain decided that Hore-Belisha must be shifted from the War Office in order to avoid a revolt of the generals in wartime.

It is doubtful whether they would have revolted. More likely, they would have continued their intrigue against Hore-Belisha behind the scenes. Here was Chamberlain the appeaser on the home front. Appeasement is a matter of temperament and not so much a policy based on the appraisal of a situation. He was going to offer him the Ministry of Information, for which Hore-Belisha was eminently suitable.

Macleod writes: "At the eleventh hour, however, this sensible and imaginative appointment was subjected to a virtual veto from the Foreign Office." He quotes Chamberlain's own record of a conversation with Lord Halifax: "He (Halifax) thought it would have a bad effect on the neutrals, both because Hore-Belisha was a Jew and because his methods would let down British prestige." It had also been suggested, Macleod says, that the appointment of a Jew would discredit the Ministry of Information in American eyes, but Chamberlain had already consulted the former British Ambassador to Washington, Lindsay, "who dismissed the suggestion at once as entirely baseless."

Yet Chamberlain dropped the original plan and offered Hore-Belisha the Board of Trade, which Belisha declined on the spot. From what we know now, it must be assumed that Hore-Belisha would have declined the Ministry of Information too.

And so at the age of forty-six Leslie Hore-Belisha became an "elder statesman." He was made a baron and settled down to writing and lecturing, returning to public life only for a brief interval as Minister of National Insurance in Churchill's caretaker government.

Macleod, a very perceptive politician, says that to Chamberlain and Halifax anti-Semitism was alien and repugnant. This may have been so, but there is no doubt that others, especially Halifax's advisers at the Foreign Office, whose views he reflected at his interview with Chamberlain about Hore-Belisha, were not free from anti-Jewish bias, though it may have been more subconscious than conscious.

It is also agreed by knowledgeable contemporaries that Hore-Belisha's Jewishness stamped him as an "outsider" among the generals, a man from the wrong side of the tracks, so to speak.

These matters were rather important in pre-war class-conscious Britain. For that matter, they still are, though perhaps to a lesser degree. This is not to say that a Jew cannot aspire to being a minister of the Crown. Many Jews have held ministerial offices, and some still do. But social snobbery, more than overt anti-Semitism, prevented Belisha, a Jew of middle-class origins, from acquiring true friends in Army circles, and without such friends there is simply no way of fighting a conspiracy. It cannot be fought by making speeches in the House or by appealing to the public. There is no way of pinpointing the intrigue. "When Belisha resigned, he found that he had no friends; this is why he never staged a comeback," a veteran Conservative statesman wrote in commenting on Minney's book.

As I write these lines, I have before me a note from Hore-Belisha. "I am going to France," it reads, "for a few days; do contact me after I return and we shall have a chat." This was in reply to a note in which I asked him whether we could meet to talk about the "Bloch plan," to see whether it could be published. Our meeting never took place. Belisha died of a heart attack in Rheims, as he was addressing a meeting of the Anglo-French Parliamentary Union. He was sixty-four.

The "Bloch plan" was named for its author, Moses Joseph Bloch, an architect and engineer of great ability and vision, in some ways bordering on genius. In the 1930's Bloch worked on a plan for a canal to connect the Red Sea with the Mediterranean. He was prompted in this ambitious scheme by three considerations: The Suez Canal, he calculated, would not be able to carry all the traffic later in the century, and an alternative canal was therefore an international necessity; Egypt was bound to gain her independence and was not to be trusted with the Suez Canal; a Red Sea — Mediterranean canal could prove a blessing to the future Jewish State, which would certainly become a reality during the century. His appraisal of the issues, from the vantage of the shortsighted thirties, was truly prophetic.

Bloch was a Lithuanian Jew with the logical and lucid mind of the *Litvak*. He had studied architecture in Milan and engineering in Germany. He worked on his remarkable plan for six years, completing it down to the very last detail, and had patented two inventions having to do with the plan. I am no expert in these matters, but it seemed to me at the time of my correspondence with Hore-Belisha that Bloch's blueprint should see the light of day, if only for its romance.

But how did Hore-Belisha enter into all this? Bloch had come to London in 1939 and met with Dr. Chaim Weizmann. The latter, however, did not show much enthusiasm for the plan and directed Bloch to Professor Selig Brodetsky, who was then the head of the Political Department of the Jewish Agency. Brodetsky, a man of vision and a fine mathematician, grasped the canal plan and its implications at a glance, but told Bloch frankly that the Zionist organization would not be able to take it up, as it was then in the throes of the fight against the White Paper.

At that time there was in London a body known as the Negev Group, whose aim was to secure a charter for the development of the Negev, either as part of the British mandated territory of Palestine or as a *corpus separatum*. To this group belonged Teddy Zissu (son of Alexander Zissu, leader of the Rumanian Zionists who was imprisoned by the Rumanians, released after several years, and died in Israel a broken man); Major Jarvis (an ex-governor of Sinai); Lord Dufferin; Frank Sanderson, M.P.; John Gwyer; and a number of other peopel, myself among them.

Bloch was my former teacher and good friend, and after his disappointing meetings with Weizmann and Brodetsky, I took him to see Teddy Zissu. As a result of this meeting, the Negev Group took over the sponsorship of Bloch's plan. Zissu and Lord Dufferin met with Hore-Belisha, who was immediately fired with the idea of an alternative canal. He told them: "There is a war coming but after the war we shall need Bloch badly; let us keep the plan for when we need it." He also received Bloch.

Of the three available copies of the plan (with the explanatory notes), one was left with Hore-Belisha and one with Zissu.

Bloch went back to Lithuania, where he perished in the Nazi holocaust. Zissu was killed in action, and his papers were burned when a bomb hit his London home. Hore-Belisha was left with the only known surviving copy. I do not know whether it was actually among his papers when he died.

Hore-Belisha was a proud Jew, though not an observing one. His wife was not Jewish, and their marriage was performed in an

Anglican church. He himself often went for periods to the monastery of the Cistercian Order, observing its vow of silence. On the other hand, he was a passionate Zionist all his life. He lived long enough to visit the Jewish State, and returned full of enthusiasm, even addressed a dinner of the Joint Israel Appeal; where he spoke as a Zionist, not as an outsider. During the great debate on the White Paper in May, 1939, he fought it inside the Government, and when he found himself in a minority, he abstained from voting for it in the House, despite extreme party pressure. (The late Walter Elliot, then Minister of Health, and a non-Jew, also abstained).

Hore-Belisha once told me that he would have resigned over the White Paper, except that it came at a time when England was on the eve of a war against Nazism and he was deeply involved in the preparations. I must confess that I was not convinced at the time that he would actually have resigned. There was his sense of mission and his ambition. (He always kept a large portrait of Disraeli in his study). But now I find myself regretting my earlier doubts. He did decline to stay in the Cabinet as President of the Board of Trade. His pride was apparently stronger and more important to him than his ambition.

Neville Laski

The Last of the Mohicans

HE NAMES OF English public offices seldom give an idea of what their holders really do. Thus, the Lord Chamberlain's real job is to license films and plays. His powers are delegated to officials of lower rank, but he is the responsible head of the office which does the licensing.

The First Lord of the Admiralty is neither a lord nor an admiral. He is a politician who serves as Minister of the Navy. And there is no Second Lord of the Admiralty. But there are five Sea Lords, of whom the first is the Commander-in-Chief of the Navy.

A recorder is not the chief of the Public Records Office. He is a judge of Quarter Sessions, which are criminal courts. He is also the chief legal officer of the city where he operates. It is all very simple, really.

The recorders of London and Liverpool rank with High Court judges. And so the appointment of Neville Jonas Laski, Q.C. (Queen's Counsel, the designation accorded to eminent lawyers by the Crown), to the recordership of Liverpool in 1956 was of more than passing interest to British Jews. For Neville Laski is one of the most distinguished and at the same time one of the most popular among them.

Laski is what one might call a "communal type," who devoted all his time and energy outside his legal work to the Jewish community. There is hardly a communal office which Laski has not from the top, having held the highest office in the community, held at one time or another — but in reverse order. He started from the top, having held the highest office in the community, that of president of the Board of Deputies of British Jews, the representative body of Anglo-Jewry, from 1933 to 1940. He was only fifty when he retired from the presidency of the Board — and started working his way downwards.

Until quite recently, on any rainy afternoon one could see the ex-president of the Board of Deputies rushing to a meeting of a subcommittee of some small organization. The reason he always

wears a shabby black overcoat and an old hat seems to be that
he cannot find time to buy himself new ones. It is still not unusual
for him to address happily a Jewish gathering numbering ten
people (counting the chairman). There is, of course, something
charming about such self-effacement.

Laski voluntarily deprived himself of all chance of playing a
part in international Jewish politics by remaining throughout the
years an isolationist, which in this context means a British Jew
who is against British Jews getting mixed up with other Jews.

He is a good Jew by all standards. He is a proud Jew. But
he is a kind of Jewish Colonel Blimp, with all the old-world
charm, all the natural dash, and all the misplaced courage of that
famous character.

Colonel Blimp regards all foreigners with suspicion. Mind you,
he would go a long way to help them when they are in trouble,
but he would cheerfully blackball them if they tried to join his
club. Laski, too, would go a long way to help his fellow Jews
in other countries, and he has done so many a time; but he
stubbornly avoids all Jewish organizations of an international
character, such as the World Jewish Congress and the British
Zionist Federation.

This is not to say that Laski is an anti-Zionist. Far from it.
The Board of Deputies was anti-Zionist before the Balfour
Declaration, and settled down to non-Zionism between the wars.
But Neville Laski was the first president of the Board of Deputies
to go to a Zionist Congress and he was the non-Zionist chairman
of the Administrative Committee of the Jewish Agency for Palestine. But the "non-Zionist" was always underscored. Here was
the escape. He did not let himself get mixed up with the real
Zionists. As a Jew he loves Zion; as an Englishman he is merely
a good friend of the Jewish State, even a friend in need, but
no more.

Neville Laski comes from the famous Manchester Laskis. His
father was Nathan Laski, the acknowledged leader of Manchester
Jews for many years. The late Professor Harold J. Laski was his
younger brother. His daughter, Marghanita Laski, is a distinguished and gifted authoress.

Laski is an Ashkenazi Jew, but this did not prevent him from
joining the Sephardi community and becoming one of their elders.
Perhaps this is a tribute to Mrs. Laski, who is the daughter of
the late Moses Gaster, scholar and *Haham* (chief rabbi) of the
Sephardi community in Britain.

Juliet Pannett.

British judges don't take an active part in political life, as a rule. But there are some non-partisan Jewish organizations left to provide an outlet for a man like Judge Laski. Neville Laski has reached the higher ranks of his profession; a judgeship is the crowning glory of any lawyer in England. But he made no impact in the legal field. Ironically enough, despite Laski's strenuous efforts to avoid involvement with international Jewry, he will be remembered primarily in *Jewish* history, or more precisely, in the Jewish chronicles of the years between the two world wars.

Wolf Mankowitz
The Hazards of Success

WHAT IS A JEWISH WRITER? Is he one who writes only in Hebrew or Yiddish? Or is he one who writes, in whatever language, exclusively about Jews? Or is he one who is a recognized and avowed Jew but writes about other people? It is not my purpose here to join in this argument. All I want to say is that Wolf Mankowitz is a recognized and avowed Jew who writes about *people,* some of them Jews and some of them non-Jews. The literary critics and historians can place him in whatever category they like — it will not worry him.

The first name is Yiddish, the surname is Russian, the shrewdness is Cockney, and the nonchalance is English upper class. All this is coupled with a brilliant mind, a facile pen, a Jewish philosophy of life, a deep understanding of human nature and, lest we forget, a Cambridge degree.

This, then, is Wolf Mankowitz, an Anglo-Jew who is a popular and at the same time significant man-of-letters in present-day England. The baby face, the stoutness, and the awkward movements — usually associated with babies before they shed their puppy fat — conceal the active and penetrating mind, which, however, comes to the fore after the first few sentences of any conversation with him.

Wolf Mankowitz is widely known as a screen writer, play producer and television personality. Millions all over the world know him as the author of those fine films, *A Kid for Two Farthings, Expresso Bongo* (which was also a stage play), *The Day the Earth Caught Fire* (for which he received a British Academy award), and other film scripts, plays, musicals, and television series. But Mankowitz himself insists — and rightly — that he is essentially a novelist; that his basic medium is the novel, and that his film scripts and plays have been merely adaptations of of his novels, or literary diversions. This claim is based on solid literary achievement. *My Old Man is a Dustman, Make Me an Offer, A Kid for Two Farthings* (a Book Society recommenda-

tion), *The Mendelman Fire,* have been variously described by
critics as "masterpieces," "in the Shakespearean comedy tradition," "in the Dickensian tradition." That Mankowitz is still
looked upon by the average newspaper reader (who hardly ever
reads a book) as a wizard in the mass media, and not as a novelist, is due to his incredible versatility.

If Mankowitz's novels are to be adapted for the film and
television screens, no one could do it better than Mankowitz himself. This is not only his own opinion, but the generally accepted
view of experts and laymen alike. Yet even Mankowitz himself
has to compromise when it comes to the visual media. He told
me, for example, that the film, *A Kid for Two Farthings,* is but
a thinned-down version of a meaningful novel, and that its real
point is probably lost on the filmgoer.

This is not by way of moaning over the vulgarity of our age.
Mankowitz is too much of a lover of people, all sorts of people,
to take a snobbish or jaundiced view of the common man and his
tastes. Unlike many others who spent their childhood in the East
End of London, Mankowitz never complains about the crude-
ness of its dwellers. He is still very much at home among them,
and they call him "Wolfie," which he obviously enjoys, since he
lets them do it in his short stories. The East End remains his
inexhaustible source of types and ideas. There is poetry amidst
all the roughness and lack of sophistication of this vast area
stretching along the Thames River from Aldgate Pump on the edge
of the City down to the Country of Essex. Mankowitz has per-
ceived and captured a great deal of it, as did Israel Zangwill
before him. Like Zangwill, James Joyce, and Sholem Aleichem,
Mankowitz elevates his local types to the level of universal characters. He has been doing with them what James Joyce did with
the Dubliners, and Sholem Aleichem with the Jews of the Pale of
Settlement. "Mankowitz is the folk-poet of London E.1," says
George Malcolm Thomson, the celebrated book reviewer of the
Evening Standard — E.1 being the postal designation of that part
of the East End of London known as Whitechapel.

Wolf Mankowitz was born in Fashion Street, E.1, in the very
heart of Whitechapel. Fashion Street is a misnomer if ever there
was one. There is nothing fashionable about it, except Mankowitz's
own writings. It is a dingy side-street, where the shopkeepers and
tailors used to live over their shops and workshops, — as late
as 1924, when this favorite son of Fashion Street was born to
Russian-Jewish parents.

Wilf Mankowitz

Juliet Pannett.

His father was a dealer "in various things," as Mankowitz himself puts it. The Old Man came to England when he was fifteen, so that he brought with him much of the Russian-Jewish tradition, which Mankowitz absorbed at home. This is where his love for Yiddish comes from. But it is a kind of unconsummated love. For Mankowitz does not know Yiddish well. He is attracted by the Yiddish lore — there is only Yiddish lore but no Yiddish learning in Whitechapel — and he harbors a nostalgia for the fruity Anglo-Yiddish which used to be the lingo of White-chapel Jews before they prospered and moved out to the more comfortable residential areas of West and North-West London and acquired English as their daily vernacular.

Mankowitz realizes, of course, that there is no future for Yiddish without Yiddish-speaking East-European Jews. But you cannot dispel a childhood romance with logical argument, espe-cially in the case of a romantic like Wolf Mankowitz.

Apart from that nostalgia for Yiddish, Mankowitz has no visible ties with Jewish life. And yet, he *is* a full-blooded Jew, who would never dream of hiding his Jewishness. He is too proud a man for that. In moments of reasoning, Mankowitz veers towards the Koestlerian Theory of the need for a personal choice between settling in Israel and voluntary, painless assimiliation. However, he is a sentimental character, not at all the type who always acts from reason or logic. The mystique of Jewishness exercises him, as it does many a Jew of his generation. He is, therefore, interested in Israel and in Diaspora Jewish life, without being involved in any kind of organized Jewish activity. Mankowitz's origins are Russian-Jewish, not Hungarian-Jewish like Koestler's. Which makes a tremendous difference when it comes to applying the Koestlerian Theory. Russian Jews of the second generation just cannot do it.

Until very recently, the life of a busy and successful writer did not absorb all of Mankowitz's time and energy. He was also a showman, having sponsored plays on the London stage, usually his own but not exclusively so. He did not seem to be able to go wrong even in this tricky business, until he incurred a failure with a musical based on a notorious murder case. The critics did not like it and the public took their advice, for a change. The piece was especially roughly handled by Bernard Levin of the *Daily Express* (known as the Kosher Butcher). Mankowitz, in-clined to be impish at all times, had two chorus girls of the play deliver a miniature coffin to Levin at the *Daily Express* offices in Fleet Street. There was Mankowitz himself leading the procession, and a host of reporters and press photographers buzzing around, with a policeman regulating the traffic. A good time was had by all, but the play was not saved. Mankowitz lost money and prestige. The spell was broken. He did not, however, take it too badly. The philosopher in him came to the rescue, and he remarked: "Perhaps it is good for my soul to be deflated a little."

As if a dual existence as a writer and a showman was not enough for one person, Mankowitz was for many years also an art dealer, specializing in precious china, on which he is a recognized expert. He had his showrooms in the Piccadilly Arcade, one of the fashionable streets off Piccadilly, which could be aptly named Fashion Street if London street names had any logic about them. The showrooms were full of both modern and antique Wedgewood. Mankowitz not only dealt in these lovely things, but also wrote about them. His *The Portland Vase and the Wedgwood Copies* and *Wedgwood* are superbly written monographs. With Reginald G. Hagger he also published *The Concise Encyclopedia of English Pottery and Porcelain.*

I once found Mankowitz in an upstairs room over his showrooms. He looked a little incongruous in his dilapidated sweater against the background of antiques and plush. There was Mankowitz the film writer defying Mankowitz the antique dealer. Film folk do wear old sweaters, but antique dealers wear white shirts and dark jackets over striped trousers. This busy office was also Mankowitz's study. He said the constant stream of people and the perpetual ringing of the telephone was stimulating. But he might move out some day, he said, and do his writing in a quieter place. Perhaps in the country, in a cottage or something; perhaps back to the East End, but it is hardly quiet there even without the Jews. The Negroes who moved in after them are not much quieter.

The East End — here was a favorite subject for both of us; it so happens that I am also an addict of the East End, though I never lived there. Mankowitz felt one must salvage as much of it as one could while the going was good — and he has done it furiously, and very well indeed. *A Kid for Two Farthings, Make Me an Offer, The Mendelman Fire, The Bespoke Overcoat* are all East End tales. Mankowitz himself considers *My Old Man's a Dustman* his best. He speaks of it with real affection. Perhaps the fascination for dustmen — there are one or two more in Mankowitz's books — is the hankering for a grand salvage operation in the colorful East End, before all its characters and all its lore, Jewish and Cockney, disappear forever. For London dust-

men not only dispose of the rubbish, they also salvage from it
whatever is still useful or interesting or valuable. "You'd be
surprised what one finds in a dustbin," one of them once told me.
Mankowitz's dustman, Old Cock, is — unlike Shaw's Doolittle
— an imaginative and resourceful type. He belongs to a different
generation of dustmen, who have their dignity and go on strike if
conditions are not satisfactory.

Mankowitz tells me that his bedside book is the Bible. Some
biblical characters fascinate him. Apart from its moral and aes-
thetical appeal, the Bible is for him also a source of characters
and ideas for his writings, as it is, and always has been, for so
many writers. But there is no getting away from the East End.
It Should Happen to a Dog is based on the book of Jonah — no
need to invent, says Mankowitz, the story is perfect — but the
smell inside the fish is that of "Billingsgate," the famous London
fish mart. For years now Mankowitz has been toying with the
idea of a play with Jezebel as the heroine. There are only three
characters in the play — Jezebel herself, King Ahab, and Elijah.
Ahab is torn between two loyalties, but Jezebel succeeds in having
her way. Her attraction as a woman is too strong for the king
and he succumbs.

Mankowitz has been translated into sixteen languags, but
Yiddish is not among them; little of his work has been translated
into Hebrew, either. There is not much money in Hebrew and
still less in Yiddish. Yet Mankowitz is mystified. Perhaps it is
difficult to render the vernacular into Yiddish or Hebrew, he
speculates. I wonder. After all, if you can "do" Whitechapel in
Italian and Japanese, how much easier it must be to "do" it in
Hebrew, and especially in Yiddish. Why, there is an excellent
Hebrew translation of Zangwill's *The Children of the Ghetto.* So
we agree that there must be some other reason — or perhaps no
reason at all. They have just not come around to it yet.

With a good wife and four healthy sons, Mankowitz seemed a
happy man all round. Apart from that musical, he had not failed
in anything since he left Whitechapel, except in his effort to lose
weight. He told the story in a hilarious series in a London evening
newspaper, and assured us at the time that it had been a complete
success. However, he seems back to "normal" these days.

How did Mankowitz find time for so much activity? There were
hundreds of short stories, in addition to the novels and plays
and films. And then there was the business, which in itself would
have been a full-time job for an active man. "Time is expandable,"

Mankowitz used to say. You kind of spin it out, if you know how.

And then, suddenly and without warning, in 1962, Mankowitz made a complete break with his mode of life and moved to Barbados, lock, stock and barrel, wife, sons, typewriter, and all. Approaching forty, Mankowitz had the courage to make a decision which has altered his whole life. He is now living quietly on that sun-drenched island, trying to be comfortable without the London amenities, and claiming to be very happy, which is obviously so. Why did he do it?

"One cold, wet autumn Sunday," says Mankowitz, "we decided to spend half of our lives among the bearded figs, coconut palms, and waving sugar cane of tropical frangipani-scented Barbados." Sounds lovely, but why?

Here is the explanation, as given by Mankowitz: "We were becoming too established in the comfortable but anxiety-ridden ruts of the affluent success world . . . The other ten million Londoners were crowding in on us."

London has, in fact, more greens and open spaces than any other big city in the world. One can live a quiet and secluded life in London if one wishes to do so. It is not London as such that caused this revolt; it is two streets in London — Shaftesbury Avenue, the street of the theatres, and Wardour Street, the center of the film industry. Mankowitz wants to do some more serious writing, but he could not keep away from the bright lights while he was within a bus ride of the alluring places. There are other people who have developed a healthy contempt for this kind of existence, but few have the courage to make a clean break.

It will be extremely interesting to see what this fine writer and very talented man will produce while leading a quiet and reflective life on a hot island. There is something Tolstoyan about this voluntary escape (and the latest photographs show that Wolf has pulled out his shirt and let it hang down, like Lev Nikolayevich). What shall we get in the way of literary works out of this one-man revolt against himself?

Lord Marks of Broughton

The Great Giver

I N THE PROCESS of elevating Englishmen to the peerage, "Public Services" is often a euphemism covering up support for the ruling party, and "charitable activities" is another one, meaning contributions to electoral funds. Only on very rare occasions is it *literally* true. The peerage bestowed on Lord Marks is such a case.

At 73, Sir Simon Marks, the chairman and managing director of Marks and Spencer, Ltd., was made a peer of the realm for public and charitable services in 1961. He became a baron, which is the lowest rung in the hierarchy of the peerage. He took the title of Lord Marks of Broughton — a peer's title must be connected with some country place, or "seat," even if he was born in an apartment in Manchester, as Lord Marks was, and Broughton is where Lord Marks has his country house.

Marks is the first half of Marks and Spencer, one of the best known and most patronized chain-store companies in the world, an institution in Britain. This is not to say that Lord Marks has not made his individual impact felt in the numerous fields of human welfare and in the various aspects of Zionism. But one cannot write about Lord Marks without saying something about Marks and Spencer. It would be rather like writing about Lord Beaverbrook without mentioning the *Daily Express*. The firm was founded at the end of the last century by Michael Marks of Leeds, father of the present Lord Marks, whose name was "canonized" in the brand name of "St. Michael," which the goods sold at Marks and Spencers bear, and which became the hallmark of good quality at reasonable prices.

Michael Marks started with a stall in an arcade. He had a good selling line — "Don't ask the price, everything is a penny." Spencer is the name of a Yorkshireman, Tom Spencer, a supplier who sold Michael Marks goods and subsequently became his partner. Mrs. Spencer died recently at the age of 99; she retained

Juliet Punnett.

her shares in the enterprise, but the controlling interest was for a long time, and remains to date, in the hands of Lord Marks and "The Family" (as the M and S people with Lord Marks at their head came to be known). The group includes Lady Marks' brother, Israel M. Sieff, who is vice-chairman and joint general manager; Harry Sacher, a fine essayist and author, whose wife is Lord Marks' sister; and sundry members of the "clan," well over a score of them.

It so happened that the annual report and accounts of Marks and Spencer, Ltd., were published a day before the chairman's elevation to the peerage. Some of the figures will give an idea of the scale on which this enterprise operates: total sales of 166,-500,000 pounds sterling in the reported year, as against 148,-000,000 pounds the year before; net profit 10,295,000 pounds as against the previous year's 9,081,000 pounds. These sales were effected in some 200 stores, all bearing the green-and-gold sign which is a familiar landmark in almost every British town and in most districts of the large cities.

There is hardly a high street in Britain without this sign over a distinctive edifice of modern, streamlined design inside and outside — clean, tidy, and hygienic — where throngs of people do their shopping in comfort and ease, buying things which range from ladies' dresses and woolen clothing to aesthetically packaged foodstuffs, from men's shirts to travel goods. There is hardly a British citizen who does not wear some sort of M and S garment; many tourists do their shopping there, too.

If Britain is a welfare state, Marks and Spencer is a welfare organization within the welfare state. Their scores of thousands of employees used to be well looked after during their working days and in sickness and old age long before the welfare state came into being. The friendly attitude of the staff towards the customers reflects this treatment, and pays handsomely in terms of profit and the good name of the firm, as the accounts show. This way of running a giant business is known as "Marks and Spencer economics," an affectionate quip by a student of Marxian economics.

The immense organization is run — perhaps "inspired" would describe it better — by Lord Marks. He knows how to delegate authority, yet controls the destinies of the enterprise himself from an elegant office in London's Baker Street.

This, then, is one aspect of Lord Marks. He is not the first

"Jewish Jew" to become a lord. Nor even the first Zionist. There is Lord Rothschild, for one, and there are others who have taken their Jewishness and their Zionism to the House of Lords. But Lord Marks is the most identified of the Jewish lords with Zionism and Israel. In his Manchester days — he is a graduate of a Manchester school and lived in that city until M and S moved their headquarters to London after the First World War — he joined Dr. Chaim Weizmann, at the time reader in organic chemistry at Manchester University, and gave him his time, devotion, and technical aid unstintedly. The business was already good enough to enable Marks to devote his time to a cause, and he had the early Zionist's zeal to give it gladly.

His influence on Zionism and his financial help to it increased as he acquired more standing and wealth, but the man was there from the beginning to devote himself to it. He acted as Weizmann's secretary and aide, and many years later described Weizmann as his teacher in Zionism. Their close friendship lasted until Weizmann's death. Lord Marks' name thus became ineradicably associated with Zionism and the upbuilding of the Jewish National Home.

Lord Marks goes about with an amused smile on his face, the smile of a philosopher who cannot possibly get excited over formal honors, and who does what he does out of a deep conviction, with no need to be fed by the flattery of his fellow men. Dark, of medium stature, looking younger than his age, neatly but not ostentatiously dressed, his hat at a rakish angle denoting individuality and refusal to conform, Lord Marks seems to find it easy to live on two levels, as a Jew and as an Englishman, simultaneously. It is take-it-or-leave-it with him, whether among non-Jews, who may resent his great devotion to Israel, or among Jews, who may fail to understand a deeply rooted Jewishness like his without synagogal practice.

Lord Marks is one of the great givers of our time. It would be difficult to add up the money he has given away to various causes. And he would be the least likely person to tell. I doubt if he ever took the trouble to figure it out in detail. But even more important than the sums involved is the art of giving, an art in which he is a pathfinder and great master, the originator of a system which some other rich men try to learn. The giving is done spontaneously, without waiting to be asked, and with an obvious willingness to share worldly possessions with those less endowed, or to contribute to the welfare and happiness of society, whether it be Jewish or general. Lord Marks shares his wealth with a sense of privilege, the way some scholars share their knowledge. "We have to learn to part with money," he advised not long ago, presumably addressing his fellow millionaires.

Berl Locker, a former member of the Jewish Agency Executive, who operated from London for a number of years, once told me that whenever the Agency was short of money for the bare necessities of organizational life, they turned to "The Family," and funds were always provided, as either loans or gifts. Very few people knew about it at the time, and it is still not generally known.

There are also the large annual donations, large even for a man of Lord Marks' means, to the United Israel Appeal, the Hebrew University, many other Israeli institutions, and local Jewish charities, all given as a matter of course — "made available" is the phrase used. And there are many private recipients of Lord Marks' generosity: perhaps an aged Zionist worker who cannot make do on his old-age pension; perhaps an Israeli who has written a book and cannot find a publisher; perhaps the son or daughter of an old associate in Zionist work who is hard up. Sometimes it is even to help somebody enjoy the good things of life, which Lord Marks himself likes in his own unobtrusive way. The Simon Marks Charitable Trust is, significantly, located in the same offices as M and S, Ltd.

The M and S organization is always at the disposal of Israel for advice and training of personnel. But not, let me add, exclusively of Israel. They once held an exhibition of office simplification techniques, freely shown to all comers, including competitors.

Lord Marks' philanthropic activities are not confined to Israel and Zionism. Such exclusiveness would not be true to his character. Many important British institutions, notably the Royal College of Surgeons, of which he is an honorary fellow, have benefited from his grants in a way that has enabled them to expand and improve their work. His help to the College is of such scope that the results, in terms of experiment and research, may well benefit humanity at large.

Lord Marks is still giving his services to Israel in a personal way. Until recently, he was the very active president of the

United Israel Appeal. He retains this office, though he is now less engaged in the day-to-day work of the Appeal. He seems to combine the running of his immense business organization with public service in both the Jewish and general spheres without much effort, all in a five-day week and a seven-hour day, and is never in a hurry. This again is an art privy to the man.

The House of Lords is, of course, a legislative body, not merely a place to honor deserving worthies. It is the Second Chamber of the British Parliament. The new Lord Marks is bound to make his mark there too. His wisdom, sagacity, feeling for human need, and enthusiasm for new ideas (some of which originate in his own mind) are a definite asset to the House of Lords. He is not a party man by temperament. A liberal in the unorganized sense, would describe his politics, whichever way he may have cast his vote in elections. (This point will not rise any more: lords and lunatics have no vote in the United Kingdom.)

Among his friends Lord Marks is counted as a good companion with a keen sense of humor and a sense of fun, a connoisseur of good jokes, a generally likeable character. It can be said of him that he enjoys not only the respect and gratitude of his fellow-citizens and fellow-Jews, but also their affection, which is, of course, a much greater achievement.

The Marchioness of Reading

The Pull of Judaism

I F WE DO NOT despair of the human race altogether, it is because there are still people with an acute social conscience who are prepared to translate urgings into action.

The Marchioness of Reading, wife of the late second Marquis of Reading, is one of these people. Her place, both in English society and among Jews, is not merely a result of her social standing. She is an outstanding personality in her own right, who would have made her mark even if she were not a marchioness.

Lady Reading pursues her political and social activities on two parallel lines that meet only in her person. In the Jewish sphere, she is president of the British Section of the World Jewish Congress, joint chairman of its European Executive, and a very active member of that body's World Executive. Years of devoted and successful work for the Keren Hayesod, Youth Aliyah, and several other Jewish causes preceded her present activity in the World Jewish Congress. In the non-Jewish sphere, she is president of the National Council of Women of Great Britain, which makes her one of the influential women in the United Kingdom — still largely a country dominated by men.

This warm-hearted, proud, and active Jewess, who occupies such a leading position in Jewish life, was brought up as a Christian. Her father, the first Lord Melchett, who had been Sir Alfred Mond before his elevation to the peerage, was a Jew and remained one all his life, but her mother was a Christian. The father did not interfere in his daughter's early education, but there came a time when he could exercise his influence in his own inimitable way, and he did.

Eva Violet Mond attended the Anglican Church with her mother, and was still a Christian when she married the son of the first Marquis of Reading, who at various times was Viceroy of India, Foreign Secretary, Lord Chief Justice, and British Ambassador to the United States.

The first Lord Reading ordered the New Testament to be torn from the Bible before him when he took the oath of office as

Viceroy of India. But his son was a less assertive Jew, and Lady Reading was married to him in a church as well as at a civil ceremony. Her husband remained Jewish, while Lady Reading was Christian. The Anglican Church does not refuse to marry couples of different faiths.

The crisis in Lady Reading's life came in 1928, when she accompanied her parents to Palestine and other places in the Middle East. Her father, Lord Melchett, took her to visit *Kibbutzim,* (communal settlements). Her mother took her to see ancient churches. The *Kibbutzim* won.

There was that moment at the ancient ruins of Babylon when Lord Melchott said to his daughter: "You see, the Babylonians have disappeared from the face of the earth, while we Jews are still here."

Something stirred in Lady Reading, something indefinable that made her feel her Jewish roots. In her case there was also a personal reason for the sudden restlessness that gripped her: the close bond with her father. Lord Melchett had great influence on his daughter, even if he did not choose to exercise it directly; and in their household, Jewishness was father's business, Christianity mother's.

The restlessness that began in 1928 crystalized into complete identification with Jewry and formal conversion to Judaism in 1936. In a person of Lady Reading's character, this step had to lead to action.

For her activities among Jews she chose the field of social welfare, a field in which she had been active before among non-Jews. Hence her attraction to Youth Aliyah and her close collaboration with Henrietta Szold. But even before her conversion, she had traveled widely on behalf of the Keren Hayesod and had campaigned on behalf of Jewish refugees.

During World War II, Rabbi Dr. Maurice Perlzweig, who had converted Lady Reading to Judaism, invited her to take part in the political work of the World Jewish Congress. Soon she was at the head of the British Section, sharing the anxiety of the war years, the anguish in the face of the catastrophe that was befalling European Jewry, and the daily chores of a political movement desperately engaged in attempting to save bodies from the Nazi hell.

Lady Reading was convinced of the proposition that when Jews are attacked as Jews they must defend themselves as Jews. She was convinced of the equally simple truth that people are respected only when they stand up and fight for their rights. Meekness and submission to terror, she felt, breeds contempt without offering respite.

To the World Jewish Congress she brought a practical mind, which could distill the essence of a problem and brush aside irrelevancies, sometimes impatiently. As chairman of a meeting, she had the knack of preventing a speaker from repeating himself without indicating that he was a windbag. Her aristocratic English upbringing and her education in languages, art, history, and literature in France and Germany have given her a broad outlook, worldly wisdom, and wide human interests. She is a very civilized woman, who never loses sight of the human aspect of a problem.

When Lord Reading was a minister in successive Conservative governments, Lady Reading's position as president of the British Section of the World Jewish Congress and member of its World Executive was often a little delicate. The World Jewish Congress did not always see eye to eye with the British Foreign Office, where Lord Reading was Minister of State.

Nevertheless, Lady Reading did not resign her offices. She is not the resigning type. Her dual capacity in those days — as the wife of a British cabinet minister and as a leader of an international Jewish organization — was a feat of lifemanship. She came through with flying colors.

There is nothing of the exaggerated zeal of the convert in Eva Reading. She wears her Jewishness naturally. She, who used to be a Christian, is now the most devoted Jewish member of her family circle, in which religious affiliations are not important and Jewishness is more a matter of habit, dormant pride, and vague sentiment.

Lady Reading confesses to a sense of loneliness within her family circle because her Jewish activities are not shared by other members of the family. But affection and natural tolerance leave no room for friction. Lord Reading himself was accustomed to "living with the World Jewish Congress," as he once put it in an after-dinner speech.

With all her flair for political activity, Lady Reading is very feminine. She once burst into tears at a conference because she felt that someone had treated her unfairly. Like all feminine women, she is not beyond using her charm to score a point when logic and strength of position fail.

Eva Reading is the kind of woman whose personality plays a decisive role in her good looks. She is good company, too.

Lady Reading has certainly made an impact on our generation; will she be remembered by future ones? I would say yes.

Yossl Rosensaft

The Art of Survival

THE NAME OF YOSSL ROSENSAFT invariably conjures up the the concept of survival of the individual and of the group.

At Auschwitz, when the notorious Hoessler came to take one of the Jewish martyrs, the scholar and teacher Dr. Jacob Edelstein, to his death and ordered him to hurry up, he retorted: "I am the master of my last moments." It can be truly said of Yossl Rosensaft that he was the master of his *first* moments after liberation, when he emerged at Belsen as the leader of the survivors and helped the liberators to save those who could still be restored to life. By the time the rehabilitation stage was reached, he was in complete charge of this effort.

Belsen was liberated by the British Army on April 15, 1945, at 7 minutes past 3 o'clock in the afternoon. Yossl Rosensaft, one the survivors, was then unknown except in his native town of Bendzin in Poland, where he had been a supporter of Labor Zionism. The born leader of men came to the fore in the hour of liberation, as if a dormant source of energy and inspiration had burst forth from the depth of his being. Death and sickness were still raging in the camp; even the battle-hardened British soldiers were stunned by the horrors and the misery. Of the 58,000 men and women freed at Belsen, 28,000 died after liberation. They were too far gone to be snatched from the clutches of death. There were still, though, 30,000 who could be saved. The British Army Medical Unit worked wonders under the command of Brigadier-General Glyn Hughes, but Yossl was indispensable to them, and to the survivors, from the first moment. He did not speak English in those days, but it mattered little. The British knew it was to him, as the representative and spokesman of the survivors, that they must talk.

A few days later, those of the survivors who could stand on their feet held a meeting to elect a chairman and a committee. Yossl was the natural and unchallenged choice for the chairmanship, and he held this office until the last Jew left Belsen on

Juliet Pannett.

September 6, 1950, although he himself could have gone from the
camp long before. He stayed on as the guardian of those who had
no place to go. To this day he still takes care of Belsen survivors,
wherever they are, and sees to it that those unable to work do
not lack the necessities of life, and even some of the comforts.

The story begins in Bendzin. When the Nazis came to the
town, Yossl together with other local Jews was sent to Auschwitz.
But he escaped and went back to Bendzin. One day he was
caught while riding on a tram — he never lacked physical courage
— and was again sent to Auschwitz. On the way, Yossl jumped
off the speeding train, landed in a river, and swam to the bank.
He then walked to a farmer's cottage, where an old Polish woman
gave him dry clothes and shelter. Soon he was home in Bendzin
once more. But his wife and child were still in Auschwitz, and
Yossl was determined to save them. Alas, he failed—and paid for
it with his own freedom. He found himself back in Auschwitz
after all, but managed to avoid the gas chambers. Eventually he
was sent with a number of other inmates to Belsen.

That was how Yossl Rosensaft found himself in Belsen on the
day of liberation. I met him there soon afterwards — a small,
compact man, with fair hair and bright blue eyes, dressed in a
pair of old slacks and a very clean white shirt. In those clothes
Yossl was outwardly a typical liberated inmate of a concentration
camp; but two minutes' talk with him revealed an extraordinary
character, a man in a million.

Life was not smooth for the survivors, even after liberation.
There were difficulties with the British, who did not understand
the liberated Jews and could not grasp why Yossl stubbornly
insisted that they be classified as Jews, and not as Poles or Czechs
or Hungarians. Yossl argued with no real power behind him, which
as a rule is a hopeless task in diplomacy. But he proved to be the
exception. The moral force behind his argument, and his own
personality, carried the day. The Jews of Belsen remained in the
D.P. camp — as Jews.

As so often happens to people who accept a challenge and
find their destiny in leadership, the stature of Yossl grew with
his responsibilities. When contacts between outside Jewish organizations and Belsen survivors were at last established, Yossl became a Jewish politician of international importance. He was
recognized as the man who created, out of misery and chaos,
the first Jewish autonomous community in modern times, a kind
of miniature republic. In a way, it was an experiment in self-

government three years before the establishment of the Jewish
State. It was Yossl who — from Belsen! — organized help for
the Haganah and dispatched large consignments of medical
supplies, blankets, and more aggressive equipment, as well as the
young men who, trained in Belsen, went to join the Israeli Army
during the war of independence in 1948.

Yossl Rosensaft's first serious clash with the British had a
bizarre character. The horror camp of Belsen had been burned
down, and the survivors had been moved to the barracks and
houses of the former German garrison. A few weeks later, the
British Commander in Chief decided that he wanted these buildings for one of the bases of the Army of the Rhine. The Jews were
offered other quarters at Lingen and Dipholz, a couple of small
towns on the Dutch frontier. Yossl did not like the idea. In any
case he wanted to see those places for himself before the move
was made. But the order had come down, and one party of
survivors was already on its way, while another was ready to
move off. Yossl popped over to Lingen and Dipholz and discovered that the quarters were dilapidated old buildings, without
light or sanitation. He rushed back and ordered the first party to
return to Belsen and the second party to unload. The survivors
moved back into the quarters from which they had been evicted
and stayed there, ignoring all orders to get out.

Yossl went on trial before a military court. He was charged
with defying orders, causing alarm and despondency, and other
crimes appertaining to the ignoring of orders in a military zone
under war conditions. It was a long trial. Yossl defended himself
— in Yiddish, with the help of an interpreter — adroitly and was
eventually discharged. The order to move the camp inmates was
forgotten.

There were other clashes with the occupation authorities, who
had mixed feelings about Yossl: he was in their way, but they
could not help respecting his courage. Then there was the case of
the *Dromit,* the first Israeli ship to come for emigrants from the
camps. It was impounded at Bremen by the Americans (Bremen
was an American outlet to the sea inside the British Zone) because they suspected that the 688 huge crates on board did not
hold merely the belongings of the emigrants. A commission of
British officers was appointed to investigate, but the survivors
managed to unload that part of the stuff which was not strictly
"goods and chattels." The ship was released. Yossl, on behalf
of the emigrants, then claimed — and received — compensation

for foodstuffs that went bad while the investigation was going on.

Perhaps Yossl's finest hour was when he told the Anglo-American Committee of Inquiry: "We shall go to Eretz Israel." When asked by a committee member what would happen if they were not permitted to go, Yossl retorted: "Then we shall go back to Belsen, Dachau, Buchenwald, and Auschwitz, and you will bear the moral responsibility for it."

That Yossl soon added to his chairmanship of the Belsen Committee the chairmanship of the Committee of Liberated Jews in the British Zone, was only a natural development. His part in absorbing into the D.P. community German Jews as well as Jews who came over from the other side of the Iron Curtain, and his care of the Exodus Jews (whom Ernest Bevin had sent back to Germany) while at the same time protesting vehemently against the act itself, are part of postwar Jewish history.

This is not second-hand information. I witnessed those incidents myself in my days as a war correspondent. I am making this point because Yossl has his detractors, and they tend to minimize his role. To be sure, Yossl is not without faults, and some of them are serious ones. He would be the last to deny it. There is that ruthless urge for power; there is the conviction that he, Yossl, is always right; there is the dictatorial impulse. But there is also the acute charitable instinct and the kindliness. There is always remorse after a violent outburst, and it is so keen that it makes him apologize very humbly the next day.

There remains a puzzling question, and one which demands an answer: Why didn't a man of Yossl's background and experience settle in Israel when he left Belsen? He once gave me the answer in an intimate conversation, as between close friends, in the early hours of the morning when people are in a confessing mood.

Yossl had chanced to visit Israel at a time when floods swamped the *Maabarot,* the temporary clusters of huts and shacks erected to house new immigrants. He found Belsen survivors, with their children, in waterlogged huts — and he raised a furor about it. This episode made a crushing impression on him: "Was there no other way except to leave these people in water?"

When I pointed out that the state itself was in a bad way and could do very little, Yossl retorted: "I know all this as well as you do. I deprived Belseners of comforts and sent their blankets to Israel when the War of Independence started, so you don't have to tell me. But there were still at the time of my visit hundreds of thousands of Israeli citizens leading a normal life in houses and flats. Could they not have taken the victims of the floods into their homes? How could they go to bed and sleep soundly, while other people's children — children! — were knee-deep in cold water?" What would one say to that?

But time is a great healer. Yossl remains a devoted Zionist and makes his own not insignificant contribution to Israel in his individual way. The Weizmann Institute is the main recipient of his support, but not the only one.

After Belsen, Yossl devoted his talents to providing for himself and his wife (Dr. Hadassa Bimko, whom he married after the war) and their son Menachem Zvi, who was born in Belsen in 1948. Applying himself to business and finance, he achieved a meteoric success. Today he is a man of substance, he commutes between the capitals of the world, and he has a unique and world-famous art collection. Yet he has not changed — he is the same good old Yossl, with his juicy Yiddish and his Jewish wisdom and lore.

Yossl does not claim to be a connoisseur of art, but he explains his passion for paintings thus: "I am trying to compensate myself for the years of misery, when beauty was only a dream." His cherished collection of Jewish liturgical objects in old silver also has its explanation: "I am holding on to a lost world by trying to keep at least some of its physical symbols. Looking at these things, I can see in my imagination the world of yesterday which was submerged like Atlantis — but in blood, not in water."

Yossl's limitless energy is of the restless kind. He is constantly on the move. One day finds him in New York, the next day in London, that evening in Paris, and that night in Switzerland. A "jump" to Rome or Tel Aviv is routine to him. He takes a trip across the globe as some people take a walk round the block before turning in.

When at home, Yossl's constant companion is the telephone. If you drop in to see him in any capital of the world, you are sure to find him with a phone in his hand. An early morning call from an unlikely place a thousand miles away is usually from Yossl, opening in his characteristic manner: "Yo, Shmuel . . ."

After having made all his business calls and having spoken to his cronies all over the world, Yossl will pick up the phone and dial the news — if it happens to be a place where such service is provided — listening and commenting at the same time. I once saw him do it twice within a quarter of an hour. When I asked why he wanted the news so soon again, he said: "Well, didn't you make the point yesterday that the world situation changes rapidly?" It is, of course, a way of allaying his restlessness, and it has become a vice with him. However, if a man must have a vice, the telephone is perhaps one of the least harmful. He told me once that, apart from the pleasure of speaking to his family and old friends, the telephone *also* has some practical uses: he never advertises, and uses the phone to promote any business that he may have in hand. He finds this medium in better taste — a proposition to which telephone companies would subscribe, but not newspapers.

I once suggested that he puts up a monument to Alexander Graham Bell in his front garden. He mused upon the idea: "You know, it might be a good proposition. Pity he wasn't a Jew. Still, after the Jews, I like the British best, in spite of all our old quarrels."

Yossl feels at home anywhere he goes, but always he carries Bendzin and Belsen within him. It is a case of Bendzin and Belsen on the inside and London, Paris, New York on the outside.

Yossl Rosensaft's contribution to the rehabilitation of the Belsen survivors has gained a place for him in postwar Jewish history. He is reliving the Belsen days all the time, and one of the results is a handsome Belsen volume, printed at Yossl's own expense, with the proceeds of the sales going to the committee of the Belsen survivors in Israel. This is not a volume of woe; there is very little about pre-liberation Belsen in it. It is a symposium on Belsen *after* liberation — its institutions, its daily routine, its educational achievements, and its lessons for the future.

There is going to be another volume. For, apart from the responsibility of leaving some raw material for the future historian of this era, Yossl feels keenly the urge to unburden himself. It is an irresistible impulse with him. In this respect he is like the proverbial old soldier, only much more so, because his experiences have left deeper scars and his chances of survival to fight another day were more unlikely. He crammed into five years enough experience to fill the lifetime of several ordinary men, and to supply the material for a Shakespearian drama.

When Dante used to take a walk in the streets of Florence, people would point to him and say: "Here goes the man who was in Hell and came back to tell the tale." In a different and more real sense, the same can be said about Yossl Rosensaft.

Lord Samuel

Statesman Turned Sage

L ORD SAMUEL'S ninetieth birthday, in 1960, was celebrated in England as a national event. The Queen sent him a warm congratulatory telegram; the House of Lords marked his birthday with a series of laudatory addresses; the London *Times* published a special article. Can any mortal in England ask for more?

Samuel is pampered by royalty and has been spoiled by the British public ever since he left active politics and, as an elder statesman, put himself above the hubbub of day-to-day affairs and political rivalries.

When Lord Samuel completed fifty years as a member of the Privy Council, soon after his eighty-ninth birthday, he was invited to a meeting of the Council in Buckingham Palace (only a few members are invited at a time). After the meeting, the Queen's private secretary asked Samuel to meet Her Majesty in the next room. When Samuel entered it, the Queen was waiting for him. She asked him to be seated, while she remained standing. Then she awarded him the Order of Merit, one of Britain's highest distinctions, reserved for men who have made an impact on the country and on their time. It was a complete birthday surprise, prepared for Lord Samuel on the Queen's own initiative. He also holds the Order of the Bath. The chain and medal of his Order are pure gold — a gift from King George V.

All political parties, as well as the public at large, regard Lord Samuel as a sage. People look up to him for guidance in time of trouble and confusion. Those of us who were privileged to attend the dinner given Lord Samuel on his ninetieth birthday heard Professor Norman Bentwich say: "You will be able to tell your grandchildren that you dined with Lord Samuel in his ninety-first year." Since Samuel lived one-third of his life in the reign of Queen Victoria, was a pupil of the great classical scholar Benjamin Jowett at Oxford, and joined the Liberal Party while William Ewart Gladstone was still alive, the link with the past is truly awe-inspiring.

Samuel still walks with a steady step. His hair is white, but his moustache is only greyish and is as vital as ever. His back is only slightly bent. In repose he looks like a man of seventy, but he insists that he feels ten years older than he did at seventy.

Herbert Louis Samuel was born in Liverpool in 1870. His father, who died when Herbert was very young, was a banker. He left a considerable fortune, which enabled Samuel to complete his studies at Oxford without material worries and to fight two unsuccessful elections in 1895 and 1900 before he got into Parliament. In 1902 he entered the House of Commons as a Liberal, and he served until 1918. He returned to Parliament in 1929 but lost his seat in the Liberal debacle of 1935.

In 1937 he was made a viscount and became leader of the Liberals in the House of Lords (where there are now more Liberals than in the House of Commons), holding this post until age compelled his retirement from office a few years ago. But he still intervenes in debates.

This is the bare outline of a lifetime of statesmanship, service, authorship, teaching (in the widest sense), untiring effort on behalf of the underprivileged, and exemplary conduct on all levels. Ultimately, Samuel reached a status where the fading of the Liberal Party no longer affected him. While his party lost its influence, his personal standing as guide and mentor continued to grow.

Today Samuel's shortcomings as politician and statesman, his blind spots, his failures, are forgotten, while his positive contributions and his virtues are extolled. Even the Zionists and the Israelis have forgotten their old scores against him and prefer to remember only his contribution to the Jewish National Home.

This is as it should be, for the balance is overwhelmingly on the credit side. But let us look at both sides of the ledger. Lord Samuel, I am sure, would not want any other assessment

A clear, lucid mind, a vast accumulation of knowledge, a capacity for administration, a sharp wit, and a flare for ironic expression are all superimposed in him upon a warm Jewish heart and an acute desire to help alleviate the lot of fellow human beings. These qualities, accompanied by a deeply-rooted sense of justice, have made Lord Samuel what he is.

Soon after entering Parliament, Samuel rose to the top ranks of the Liberal Party, and he remained there until he retired from active politics. Those were the days when England's two-party system of parliamentary government was operated by the Tories (or Conservatives) and the Liberals. The Labor Party had not

Samuel
Nov 1941

Juliet Pannett.

yet displaced the Liberals as the other major party and thus the alternative choice of the British people.

At 35 Samuel was Under-Secreaary in the Home Office: at 39 he had a seat in the Cabinet as Chancellor of the Duchy of Lancaster (an ancient office whose holder may perform any cabinet chore); at 40 he was Postmaster General; at 46 he was Home Secretary, a post he occupied again briefly after his return from Palestine, where he served as High Commissioner from 1920 to 1925. He was the conciliator of the general strike of 1926, and he performed many other services for the Crown and the country.

Samuel never took an active part in the day-to-day affairs of the Jewish community — from the outset he was much above such chores — but he always identified himself with it. Many years ago he joined a London synagogue, where he still worships. He represented the Jewish community when his presence was required. He was the chairman of the Council for Jews from Germany, a fund-raising body for Nazi victims. His last great service to the community was performed when he accepted the presidency of the Anglo-Jewish Tercentenary Committee in 1956.

Samuel was closely identified with much of the social legislation Britain enacted in the first two decades of this century, and he is properly described as one of the founding fathers of the welfare state in the United Kingdom. He showed less sagacity in foreign affairs. The late Vladimir Jabotinsky once said that Samual was never able to see ahead clearly in foreign affairs. To some extent, this was true.

There is, for instance, the famous memorandum of a conversation between Lord Samuel and Lord Halifax in the early days of Hitler. Samuel is on record as having said that Hitler might not be as bad as was feared.

Jabotinsky's appraisal of Samuel's short-sightedness in foreign affairs was made long before that Halifax-Samuel conversation. Another instance is Samuel's disparaging statement about Winston Churchill in 1934, "Churchill is running amok in search of arms." However, British statesmen are never called to account for errors of judgment, much less for statements proved wrong in the fullness of time.

Samuel's relations with Zionism were much more complicated. He began his sustained effort to enlist British support for it on his own initiative some time before he met Dr. Chaim Weizmann in 1914. After their meeting, Samuel placed all his influence and prestige at the disposal of the Zionist leaders and made their cause his own. The then Prime Minister, Herbert Asquith, did not like it. In 1914 he wrote, "Samuel remains a Jew of the Jews, descendant of Abraham, proud and aloof and stubborn. However, he is courageous and diligent, and has a good heart."

Samuel never argued with anti-Semites, not even subconscious ones like Herbert Asquith, in whose Cabinet he served. He dismissed them with contempt; hence Asquith's reference to "pride."

After World War I, Samuel often advised Weizmann in his negotiations with the British. When Samuel was appointed the first High Commissioner of Palestine by the then Prime Minister, David Lloyd George, the Jews placed high hopes in him. He came to Palestine as a Jew, and he worshipped in the famous Churvat Rabbi Yehuda Hechassid synagogue in old Jerusalem. Pious Jews used to stand up and and recite, "And no stranger shall accede to his throne" (King David's), as the Jewish High Commissioner mounted the steps of the *Bimah* for *Maftir*.

The creation of Jordan under Emir Abdullah; the 1922 White Paper; the constant attempts to lean over backwards in order to help and appease the Arabs, who mistook kindness for weakness, as they invariably do, all brought Samuel into conflict with the Zionists. Yet, his tenure of office saw great advances in the upbuilding of the Jewish National Home. In later years, Samuel opposed the Passfield White Paper of 1930 and the MacDonald White Paper of 1939, but he rejected the "Biltmore Program" of the Zionists (which demanded statehood) as "impractical" — again that inability to look far ahead. He also opposed the partition of Palestine into Jewish and Arab states and produced his own plan for cantonization. But when an Israeli legation was opened in London, Samuel was the first to come and sign the visitors' book.

By this gracious gesture Lord Samuel made his peace with the State of Israel. His support for the Hebrew University from the day it was founded until today, has been wholeheatred and effective. He is a governor of the University and the president of the British Friends of the Hebrew University — the only public office he retains in his nineties.

As High Commissioner, Samuel went to Israel with an entourage and came back alone, as it were. Lady Samuel returned a devoted Zionist and openly expressed her disappointment at not being able to live in Israel. She continued to study Hebrew and took an active interest in Zionist affairs until her death in 1959. Edwin Samuel, heir to the title, lives in Israel. David

Samuel, Edwin's son, is at the Weizmann Institute. (Lord Samuel has two other sons and a daughter).

Samuel is also a philosopher who has carved for himself a niche in modern thought. He is perhaps more a political scientist than a philosopher in the classical sense, but he has written several philosophical books which are outside the sphere of political science proper, and for many years he served as president of the Royal Institute of Philosophy. His main aim in philosophy has been to seek a synthesis between the sciences and the arts, to draw attention to the junction where the two meet and where the humanist can exercise his influence to channel the achievements of the scientist to the uses of peace and human welfare. He has refused to cultivate metaphysics, and describes himself as a "meliorist" — a man who believes that the present is on the whole better than the past and that he future can be better still.

These ideas are developed in Samuel's books, *Belief and Action, In Search of Reality,* and other works, long and short. He has also compiled a book of quotations, in which many items are marked "H.S." — standing for Herbert Samuel.

Living on two levels — the general and the Jewish — has been no strain on Samuel. There has never been any conflict between his Jewishness and his Englishness — his is too integrated a personality to suffer from a split mind. He has never apoligized for his Jewishness. Take it or leave it, was always his attitude. They took it.

Zalman Shneur

The Samson of Jewish Letters

I T IS CUSTOMARY to talk about the three poets-royal of modern Hebrew literature — Bialik, Tschernichovsky and Shneur — ranking them in that order. Bialik occupies a unique place in Hebrew letters and in the Jewish national consciousness; some day, there may be a revaluation in regard to the other two. Such revaluations sometimes take place long after the death of an author, and Shneur died only three years ago, in 1959.

Of the three, Shneur is the only one who had two separate and distinct careers in Jewish literature — he is one of the greatest Hebrew poets and one of the greatest Yiddish novelists. In this respect he is unique and incomparable. For, Mendele Mocher Seforim, who also wrote Hebrew and Yiddish, merely re-created his own works in the other language. One thinks of Shneur as a literary phenomenon in terms of two rivers flowing from a single mighty source — one with the sweep of a Mississippi and the other with the impetus of a Dnieper.

Zalman Shneur was born in 1887 in Shklov, Russia. His father, a scion of the Shneursons of Hassidic fame, was a businessman. He was an expert on precious stones and objects d'art, but there was not much scope for such a talent in the Shklov of those days. There were seven children in the family — six sons and one daughter; Zalman was the fourth child. In his autobiographical notes, Shneur speaks of his father with respect but hardly mentions his mother. It is obvious that he had an unhappy childhood, probably due to his mother, and that this colored his attitude towards women for the rest of his life. I recall a casual remark of his which was quite revealing. We were sitting at a table outside a Paris café, when a strikingly beautiful woman went by. Shneur looked her up and down and said with a deep sigh: *"Ah, weiber, weiber, ich hob sei lib un ich hob sei faynt"* ("Women, women, I love them and I hate them").

He sometimes spoke of his wife with affection, but invariably it was in connection with her assistance in collecting material for his Yiddish novels, especially *Der Keisser un der Rebbe* (The Czar and the Rabbi). Joseph Leftwich, one of Shneur's close friends, told me that Mrs. Shneur was very patient with her quick-tempered husband. Shneur would lose his temper and complain in his articulate way; Mrs. Shneur would quietly leave the house; he would go on talking without noticing her departure — until he would suddenly see through his ground-floor window that she was outside, whereupon he would go back to his writing. He liked to travel alone, which is why many of his friends and acquaintances outside the States never met his wife.

Shneur had a built-in mistrust of women, but he was a manly man and needed their company. "It would be torture to read to an audience composed of men only," he once remarked. Always that love-hate complex. I dwell on this aspect of Shneur's character because it helps us to understand those of his poems in which women appear, as well as the heroines of his novels. The elemental force in the female of the species, like all elemental forces, fascinated him, but it also disturbed him. To be sure, he was not the unsuccessful male. A man of his imposing appearance, achievement in letters, and astringent wit had no difficulty in managing women, but he was always aware of their fickleness — their perfidy, he would call it — and kept a barrier of cynicism between himsef and them.

Zalman Shneur left home early in life. At thirteen he turned up in Odessa and tried to get his early poems published, but the going was tortuous and hunger was threatening. Bialik recognized the budding talent but could do little to help; he was himself poor at the time. A year later Shneur returned home, sick and disappointed. "I achieved nothing on the Black Sea," he relates in his autobiographical memoir.

But he soon left home again, never to go back. Warsaw was his destination. There, after the usual struggles of a young and poor man trying to break through in the field of letters, at eighteen Shneur published his first book of poetry. It was an immediate success, but he was cheated by his publisher, and he never forgot it. For the rest of his life he harbored a hatred of publishers, and he never missed a chance to lash out at them — in print, in conversation, and in correspondence.

Juliet Pannett.

Here I can draw upon my own experience. As a young man I was on the editorial staff of a large and prosperous Yiddish paper in which Shneur published *Der Keisser un der Rebbe* and *Noah Pandre* in installments. He was well paid but, of course, not well enough. Most of the chapters arrived at the office accompanied by notes on the iniquities of the publishers of the paper, notes which I enjoyed enormously. One of those missives — I translate from the Yiddish — began as follows: "My dear Goldsmith, tell those herring merchants, those bloodsuckers, those bug-ridden morons that I am not going to feed them my stuff for their lousy few sous." (He lived in France at the time.)

On another occasion he wrote, in Hebrew: "I hope you realize, young man, that I am sending you here a treasure. Take good care of it. Don't you dare print it until your accursed managers send me a cheque as per my statement — which, I am sure, they can't even read."

I wrote back to say that I was treasuring not only his manuscripts but also his letters, which I might publish one day. To this he replied, on a Hebrew postcard: "Do, do, but remember I own the copyright."

Alas, the precious Shneur file remained in Kovno. I was too stupidly honest to have filched it from the office.

To go back to the Warsaw days, the breakthrough was made, even though the fees were stolen, and Shneur established himself as a Hebrew poet of vast and unusual talent. Bialik said of him that he was like a Samson whose locks had grown over night. And Shneur's pride increased with his fame, but every new poem justified it — unless there is no excuse for that particular deadly sin.

Warsaw-Berlin-Paris-New York was Shneur's route across the Diaspora. He taught himself a great deal, and he also studied at various institutions of higher learning. Like the rest of his generation who came out of the Pale of Settlement into the wide world, he absorbed Western culture, but he was never intimidated by the West; he looked upon it with grave suspicion, and he warned again and again that the civilized veneer was only skin deep. Long before the Nazis were dreamt of, Shneur wrote his poem, "The Middle Ages are Returning." With prophetic intuition he foresaw the moral collapse of the "Nation of Poets and Thinkers." He was disgusted with the world as he saw it — and in this respect he spoke for many of us — but he refused to turn from it and lock himself up in an ivory tower, or to run away to a desert, as he put it. He kept hammering at the world, castigating it, exposing it, ridiculing and shaming it.

Yet he loved life and the good things of life; and he loved nature, the changing seasons, God's creatures, with whom he had an almost uncanny affinity. I once said to him that he seemed to prefer animals to humans, and he retorted: "Of course, naturally, how long did it take you to discover it?" And he went on to explain how superior the jungle was to the world of man.

So there were compensations for living, and there was the burning curiosity to see where the world was going. Alas, this is not given to us in one lifetime.

There is a poignant poem in which Shneur says that life is not worth shedding tears over, yet one would have liked to be able to live on and on, and one regretted that the world, such as it is, will go on after one's own demise.

Shneur came to Eretz Israel, and later to the State of Israel, very often, but he never settled there. And yet, he was less of a Diaspora Jew than either Bialik or Tschernichovsky, who did. He disliked intensely the complex-ridden Diaspora Jew, though he did not blame him for this trait. At the same time, he saw the light that was there, in the Diaspora, whether it be his own Shklov or Vilna, about which he wrote his famous poem. In his revulsion against Diaspora life, Shneur sought consolation in a Noah Pandre, the rare Diaspora Jew who knew how to hit back. Even his *Shtadlan,* Notte Notkin, is a dignified Jew who does not cringe. This is why Shneur has such appeal for the Sabras. On his part, he understood them. In the "Burden of Albion" he even came to be their spokesman and argued forcefully on their behalf. They responded by never considering him an outsider, a *Golah* poet.

Shneur in his writings spans the two national languages and the two parts of Jewry. I believe no writer of Shneur's depth and range in world literature ever achieved such natural bilingualism, as did Shneur in Hebrew and Yiddish.

People often compain that Shneur was a "difficult man." There are countless stories about his "rudeness," some of them true. Yet he was not one of those "impossible" poets who should be read and not seen. There was magic in his personality, sparkle in his conversation, and charm in his defiance of the conventions.

I have a postcard from him which begins as follows: "My dear Goldsmith, to hell with you!" (In his Yiddish original — and I

cannot forego quoting this gem — "Mein lieber Goldsmith, a
beiser yor oif dir!") All because of a typographical error in a
story by the master which was published in the newspaper I was
associated with. I had nothing to do with the proofreading, of
course. But what did it matter? Who could have been annoyed with
an epistle opening thus? Other people have had similar letters from
Shneur. They told me of the same reaction: the brilliance of the
invective made them forget the insults. After all, manners are
meant for ordinary people.

Shneur's story about Nathanya — where, he declared, he was
treated to long speeches plus cold tea without sugar is a classical example of the calculated and choice insult in his inimitable
style, which was a joy to connoisseurs — and these included most
of the victims. As a matter of fact, the speeches were long, but
the tea was excellent and sugar he declined. Again, though, what
difference did it make?

Shneur did not suffer fools gladly, but with others he "made
up" without going through the embarrassing routine of apology.
Another of his pet aversions was persons generally known —in
bad Hebrew, too — as *Am horatzim*. This designation is usualy
applied to Jews who are not well up in Jewish knowledge, the
Scriptures, Hebrew. I heard him once say that he did not at all
mind *Am horatzim* who stuck to their own business, people like
his Noah Pandre, whom he loved, but that he hated those who
tried to lay down the law to others (*"sogn deyes,"* was his term
for it). He used to pull out all the stops in telling them where
they get off.

But to quarrel with a writer of Shneur's caliber about middle-
class manners was quite beside the point. He possessed enough
talent, *esprit,* and personal charm to endow a dozen of his detractors and make them all important men of letters. In the sixty
volumes of Shneur's writings there is hardly a single mediocre
piece.

Shneur was a superb reader of his own works, and especially
of the Yiddish novels. He had the presence — an imposing
figure, a large, well-shaped head adorned by that famous beard
— and he had the art. He would act out every character — including the Mume Feige, the original jam-maker — and could
thus hold a large audience spellbound for as long as he cared to
read. Like Kreisler, he used the device of leaving a -couple of
short, striking, and especially appealing pieces for the encores.

Unlike Kreisler, he was always gloomy and testy after the tremendous ovation at the end of the evening.

Shneur asked not to be eulogized after his death — he wanted no *Hessped*. It was not that he was too modest. He was never afflicted with the self-doubt of Rabbi Nachman of Bratzlav, who asked his followers to burn all his writings after his death. Shneur simply could not bear the idea of someone appraising him without his being present to know what was being said. He could not rely on anyone else to do justice to the theme.

In one of his early poems there is an explanation of why eulogies would seem trite and hopelessly inadequate. In rough translation: "You don't mourn a rock, a rock of ages, that had stood there proud and lonely and then tumbled into an abyss."

I would hate to defy his request without being able to receive one of his admonishing and insulting letters. I hope this is *not* a *Hessped*.

Abba Hillel Silver
A Leader in Limbo

HE MAN WHO is perhaps the greatest living American Jew is not of American birth. Abba Hillel Silver was born in Lithuania in 1893, and came to America as a young boy in 1902. This is a commentary on Diaspora Jewish life. It is also a commentary on the structure of American society.

I have just now committed myself to the proposition that Abba Hillel Silver is at the very least one of the greatest living American Jews. I hasten to add that I have never belonged to Silver's following, though my press clippings include several interviews with him, one or two of them quite revealing ones, and my private papers contain numerous notes jotted down for future reference. This I say not in justification of writing this profile — there is enough Silver material available for half a dozen books — but to make quite a different point: Silver is one of those leaders who command the loyalty of their followers and assistants, friends and advisers, to a degree that leaves no room for an objective critical appraisal. Herzl had this quality; Weizmann had it; Ben-Gurion has it. Among non-Jews Churchill, Montgomery, and De Gaulle are in this category.

It remains one of the mysteries of modern Jewish life why a man and leader of Silver's stature, devotion, and scope, working within the largest Jewish community in the Diaspora, should be kept in cold storage, as it were, by the Prime Minister of the State of Israel. The mystery becomes deeper, and the sense of waste sharper, when one remembers that Ben-Gurion and Silver have seen eye-to-eye in the past on a number of basic issues, and that their recorded opinions are not dissimilar even today on the issues that matter most, such as the attitude towards Soviet Russia, Arab policy, and the security of Israel.

One can see why the timid are suspicious of Silver. They take out on him the frustrations of their own timidity. One can see why many of the common or garden variety of American and European Zionist leaders dislike Silver. This is the proverbial

Juliet Pannett.

dislike of the ignorant for the knowledgeable; they dislike them even more than the poor dlslike the rich. But why Ben-Gurion? He seems to have a "love-hate" complex about Silver, in which the "hate" comes to the fore, while the "love" remains a grudging admiration, never to be mentioned in public.

Is it because Silver still insists upon the distinction between a Zionist and a non-Zionist? Is it because Silver has always been looked upon as the most important and articulate spokesman in the Diaspora for the private-enterprise sector of Israel's economy? Is it because of Ben-Gurion's hidden fear, perhaps not even admitted to himself, that Silver might somewhere along the line of Jewish history outshine him on some occasion? Or is it because of a nagging suspicion that future historians might divide the credit for the vision of a Jewish state when Jewish fortunes were at their lowest ebb, and give some to Silver and others?

There may have been some personal friction of a more humdrum nature between these two men which we don't know about and which would in any case be too trivial to be analyzed — except by a professional psychoanalyst — if we did know. As so often happens, all these elements, and some others too, probably combine to create this paradox in Jewish life, the paradox of the Jewish State combing the Diaspora, searching for support and succor in every nook and corner of the dispersion, yet stubbornly refusing to make use of the source of Jewish and Zionist energy that is represented by Silver.

It was somewhat unusual for a *Litvak* (the designation for a Lithuanian Jew in Jewish lore) the son of a *Litvak,* as Abba Hillel Silver is, to enroll at the Hebrew Union College. Here was a natural Zionist going off to a hotbed of anti-Zionism, not to mention a different brand of Judaism (Reform) — Cincinnati.

There is a charming story in circulation that Abba Hillel Silver — and his brother Maxwell — went to Cincinnati in order to convert the then anti-Zionists of the college to Zionism. It is probably apocryphal, like most good stories. The real reason may have been the urge to shed the "Ghetto"; or it may have been the lure of the "West" to a young man from an "Eastern" home. It may have been a feeling that if one was to be a guide and mentor to American Jews, one could not do so in the idiom of an East European type of rabbi. Whatever the reasons, it was certainly a case of *"M'toch Shelo Lishma Ba Lishma"* (an action leading to an unexpected but positive result). Silver eventually played a decisive role in converting a stronghold of anti-Zionism into a Zionist center.

Ohio always was and still is to Silver both a starting point and a retreat, like the home state of many a national figure in American life. His influence at the height of his Zionist career reached out across the whole of the United States and beyond, to the whole of the Zionist world and to Eretz Israel.

With the decline in Jewry's fortunes during the thirties and forties, *Shtadlanut* (roughly, pleading without the power to back the plea) crept back and began once more to take the place of statesmanship. In a cruel and heartless world, Jews were pleading for consideration on the grounds that they had suffered so much. I remember how pleased Zionist leaders were when a well-meaning important *Goy* said in 1945 that "something would have to be done for the Jews." They were soon, however, told by Ernest Bevin that the Jews "must not push themselves to the head of the queue." Silver was one of the few who realized in time that Jews still possessed some bargaining positions and had to use them if they were not to fall by the wayside. Resistance in Palestine was one of those positions, and Silver supported it. The power of American Jews was another, and Silver did not hesitate to employ it, often daringly, and in most instances effectively.

In this struggle, he did not hesitate to embarrass Britain. I remember a British politician once telling me that Silver was "causing trouble because he is anti-British." When I pointed out that he was not anti-British, actually, but pro-Jewish, my English friend retorted: "This is a new one on me. You mean single-minded pro-Jewishness, to the exclusion of all other considerations? No Jew can get away with it." To stop the futile argument, I used the time-honored cliché, "You'd be surprised." As a matter of fact, he soon was surprised, and he said so. When I wrote some months later that the methods of Sir Moses Montefiore suited the days of Queen Victoria, my friend sent me a post card from an Arab capital, saying: "Alas, you seem to be right."

But this approach was startling even to some Jewish leaders. Indeed, Silver spent more energy in persuading Jews than he did in converting non-Jews to the idea that the Jews could no longer be trifled with. It even reached a point where Silver had to address a meeting of the American Jewish Conference in 1943 on "borrowed time." To the credit of the American Jewish Congress, they gave him their delegate's time. He swayed the delegates in favor of the creation of a Jewish state.

Looking back now, it seems incredible that people should have been so purblind at the time, but such is human nature. There was even a time, not so long ago, when British Zionists stubbornly opposed a proposal to invite Silver to address the annual dinner of the United Palestine Appeal (as it was still designated for reasons of convenience, though this was after the establishment of the State of Israel). Silver never came. Even now they don't want him, although they are scraping the bottom of the barrel for speakers and have used up everybody who might be expected to make a good speech.

This business has nothing to do with the Ben-Gurion — Silver relationship; it is simply a case of flunkies trying to outdo their masters, without understanding what the masters are really after.

Silver's mistrust of Roosevelt. in Jewish matters was at the time ascribed by Zionist leaders — at any rate by European and Palestinian ones — to the fact that Silver was a Republican. It was not until the disclosure, after the death of the president, of Roosevelt's secret letter to Ibn Saud that Silver's position was vindicated. I have never heard of any Zionist Leader apoligizing for his error in this connection. Silver too does not like to admit his own mistakes in public. But in Zionist foreign politics, which mattered most in the case of a Zionist leader in the Diaspora before 1948, he was mostly right. Besides, two failings do not make one merit.

At the Zionist Congress of 1946 in Basle, Silver was named chairman of the Political Committee. This was a decisive move on the part of those who had come to the conclusion that Weizmann must go because there was no more room for negotiation with the British. Silver and Ben-Gurion teamed up to oust Weizmann and succeeded, though only by a slim margin.

I remember well that famous night session. We left the hall on a cold, bleak morning with the knowledge that Weizmann had departed from the scene. We all felt sorry for him, but few of us regretted the results of the vote. Ben-Gurion became the unchallenged leader of the *Yishuv* (the Palestine Jewish community). It was a combination aimed at filling the gap left by Weizmann, though Ben-Gurion's and Silver's adherents eyed each other with suspicion. But there was a national emergency, and party politics had to wait.

Some people will tell you that Silver's finest hour was his oration at the American Zionist Conference of 1943. Others will

tell you that it was his address at the close of the Zionist convention of 1947. His address before the United Nations Special
Political Committee on Palestine must surely rank among his
greatest performances. Alistair Cooke, one of the outstanding
reporters of our time, who was not involved in this issue, described the speech in the *Manchester Guardian* thus: "Dr. Silver
put the case for the Jewish Agency with so much point and au-
sterity that his address became a memorable occasion." And
later on: "Dr. Silver reluctantly accepted the United Nations
partition plan on behalf of the Jewish Agency. He protested
against the suggestion of a two-year transition between the old
and the new regime and stated that if Britain withdrew from
Palestine the Haganah would leap into the breach."

That last sentence reflects the concept of basing demands upon
real power. Silver did not hesitate to warn the non-Jews about
the use of power. They took note of his warning, and it soon
turned out not to have been an empty boast. Silver also played
a part in canvassing for votes for the partition decision at the
Assembly. An English diplomat compained at the time that
"Silver isolated the British delegation."

Platform oratory calls for a different technique from addressing a committee of an international organization. Silver is also
one of the few great living orators in Jewry, perhaps the greatest
since Jabotinsky died. He has the imposing presence, the voice,
the command of language, and the ability to establish a rapport
with his audience in the early, pianissimo stages of a speech. As
he leans forward and invites attention with that famous phrase
of his, "My good friends," he has the audience eating out of
his hand. "My good friends" occurs in almost every speech of
his. But it is not so much a device as an instinctive declaration of
regard for his listeners. At any rate; it sounds completely natural,
and seems to stem from a liking for people.

Silver not only knows Hebrew but is a *Talmid Chacham* (an
acknowledged possessor of Jewish learning). He is not only a
great expert on Jewish affairs but applies to Jewish problems an
original mind nourished by vast learning. He has also proved
himself to be an adequate administrator and a shrewd man of
affairs. His contribution is not a matter of controversy. That
Kfar Silver, the Israeli village bearing Abba Hillel Silver's name,
is the creation of the Zionist Organization of America, not of the
Jewish Agency as a whole, and that he is a freeman of Ramat Gan,

where the General Zionists always had influence, is merely a commentary on party politics in Israel and Zionism.

I happened to be in Israel during one of Silvers visits. I was staying with an old friend in Ramat Gan on the day of Silver's arrival in the town. The hundreds of people who cheered him in the streets were not all General Zionists. In fact, I doubt whether the General Zionists ever had that many followers in Ramat Gan.

"But why does he not settle here?" asked a young man in a white shirt and khaki shorts. This is what many have asked in recent years. I have read somewhere that Silver's father went to Jerusalem and died there at a ripe old age. Must we wait until Silver is eighty before he goes to Israel? — is a natural question.

Jews certainly have the right to ask such a question of a deeply committed Zionist leader, a man who, while a good American, knows his Bialik as well as his Walt Whitman, his Sholem Aleichem as well as his Mark Twain. Only Silver himself knows the answer. And perhaps even he doesn't know. Perhaps it is a vague feeling that there would be no room for him to play his part; that membership on the Zionist Executive at this stage is not fulfilment for a man with greater ambitions.

At the same time, it would be unfair to say that Silver sees a need for Zionism in the Diaspora in order to rationalize his own position. There is force in his argument, and it should be dealt with on its merits. Of course, man's subconscious mind is always there, affecting all his actions. But such subconscious impulses must not be used as an argument against an individual. For they are beyond his control. Silver's ideas about Zionism in the Diaspora, as well as his distinction between Zionists and non-Zionists — in which he differs from Ben-Gurion so clearly — must be treated without reference to his own private choice between America and Israel for his domicile.

Living on two levels is no strain for a man like Silver. Only timid and apologetic Jews feel tension in such an existence. It is characteristic of Silver that he addresses a Zionist gathering on general politics in the same manner as he speaks to a convention of politicians or foreign policy experts. Not long ago he was telling a Zionist conference that Americans must learn to live with the Soviet people, since they are on the same globe. What is more, the non-Jewish press reported it quite matter-of-factly. Here was a distinguished American guiding his fellow-citizens in the complexities of U. S. — U. S. S. R. relations.

Silver once said: "A glorious radiance will always shine over the heads of this generation. Future ages will look back upon this period of Jewish history with pride and nostalgia." It must also be left to future historians to fix Silver's final place in Jewish history. By way of providing them with a little more material, I am tempted to add a purely personal impression of the man, gleaned from casual meetings and observation from the wings, as it were.

I remember a bright, warm morning in Zurich during a session of the Zionist Actions Committee. I was strolling with the late Daniel Frish, when he spotted Silver at a table outside a coffee house. We joined him. Frish, an intense and single-minded Zionist, brought up some Zionist problem, but Silver diverted the conversation to the influence of Aramaic upon Hebrew. The late Elihu D. Stone came along and joined us, and we all listened in rapt attention to a fascinating discourse on the Aramaic theme. Silver's table talk is a rare treat.

Suddenly Silver interrupted himself. "Is it time for the meeting?" Even Frish was moved to say that there was no hurry.

Silver's opponents dislike him intensely. There is always a tinge of the fanatical in their talk of him. Few remain neutral to leaders of Silver's type; people either love them or hate them.

A word is in order here about the Silver-Neumann relationship, which has played an important part in American and world Zionist politics over a period of many years. Emanuel Neumann is a Zionist leader of great distinction. He is also a Zionist thinker of no mean stature. And he is a better writer than Silver. But he early realized that Abba Hillel Silver had that additional spark, that undefineable quality, which makes a man a leader of men. Once this is accepted, there is no room for jealousy or rivalry. Friendship and mutual loyalty can then take over unhampered. Silver respects Neumann's sagacity and judgment, and draws upon it often. The Herzl — Nordau partnership, though in a different key, was more or less of the same nature. Nordau never "represented" Herzl; nor did he bask in Herzl's reflected glory. He had his own undisputed place in the partnership. And so it is with Silver and Neumann.

I doubt whether Silver will come back to active Zionist leadership. It is true, time is a great healer, but time also piles up the years. However, Silver's contribution is already made, though not fully evaluated.

Juliet Pannett.   Sydney Silverman

Sidney Silverman
Never Say Die!

IT IS SOMETIMES said that the House of Commons is the finest club in the world. In this club, some members are liked and respected, some are liked but not respected, and some are respected but not liked.

Sydney Samuel Silverman belongs to the last category. This is not to say that S.S.S. is not a likeable man. Far from it. He is companionable, witty, intelligent, and extremely well informed. But in that particular club he is not a favorite. He is a shade too articulate, a bit too pungent, a little too clever, much too logical, much too convinced of the soundness of his own principles, for this particular assembly.

Government by argument is the way of British · democracy, and the House of Commons is the arena where the argument takes place. Nevertheless, those who govern find it tedious when the argument becomes too long and their shortcomings. are too heavily underscored.

The official opposition, whether it be Tory or Labor, accepts the principle that the other side must carry on the business of government, and never forgets that next time it may be their party that will have to carry on.

Not so the individualists on either side of the House, of whom Silverman is one of the most vociferous and perhaps the most daring. He stands his ground in the face of shouts and jeers from other members and, despite attempts by the Speaker to cut him short, fights the issue out to the last fine point.

His incomparable knowledge of parliamentary procedure and the lucidity of his exposition come to his aid. The Speaker finds it difficult to keep him in check. Again and again Silverman will jump up from his seat, his small body tense, like a boxer returning from his corner, his mane of white hair flowing, his bearded chin thrust out in defiance, and his rasping voice cutting the air: "Mr. Speaker, Sir!"

The timid, the respectful of authority, the devotees of the Establishment, the haters of unpopular causes, do not like this type of parliamentarian. He disturbs their peace of mind; sometimes he even makes them wake up with a start from a comfortable nap on the green leather benches. He is almost "un-English" to them. So are one or two other members, but these are not Jewish, while Silverman is, and assertively so.

Thus the "un-Englishness" assumes a definite color — and a very familiar one. Not that anyone would dream of practicing open anti-Semitism in the House of Commons. But there is the Smoking Room gossip, which is also an institution. Sometimes it only amounts to a drop of acid in the voice when Silverman is discussed — and he is discussed a great deal.

Respect is, of course, in a different category of human relationships from affection. Silverman is respected because he knows what he wants to say and knows how to say it. He is an expert on several subjects: foreign affairs, the Middle East, the Far East, the cotton industry, British law. The expert is all the more respected in a place where expert knowledge is not the pass of entry. And who does not respect courage? Sometimes this respect even turns into grudging admiration.

Silverman's greatest parliamentary achievement, and one which has made him a national figure, is perhaps his Private Member's Bill for the abolition of the death penalty.

The argument for and against capital punishment is still raging in Britain. The well-known pros and cons have been worked to death by both sides. There is even a national committee which organizes the abolitionists and presses their views.

But the Government did not take the initiative on the issue. It was left to Silverman both to introduce and to pilot the bill through all its stages but the final one. A task like this is most difficult under the best circumstances; in this instance it was much more difficult and exacting. Passions ran high, and formidable lawyers ranged themselves against the bill. At the last moment, the Government presented their own bill for partial abolition. Though only a partial victory, it was a great personal triumph for S.S.S.

S.S.S. champions abolition because he sincerely believes that murderers are not born but made by society, that almost all of them are victims of circumstance and not persons with an innate inclination to kill. There is also, of course, the possibility of a miscarriage of justice. Here is S.S.S. the Socialist at his best, the man who sees society in terms of naves and have-nots, of privileged and under-privileged.

Sydney Samuel Silverman was born in Liverpool 67 years ago. His father came to England from Yassi, Rumania, and worked in textiles. On his mother's side he is a third-generation Britisher. His mother's mother was born in Birmingham, his mother in Manchester. S.S.S. graduated from Liverpool University and took a post as English Lecturer at the State University of Finland in Helsinki.

After a few terms he came back, opened a law practice with a capital of twelve pounds, and soon became a well-known solicitor in the North of England. He did not transfer his office to London until recently. A very good lawyer, he could have made a fortune if he had not entered politics. But enter it he did, in 1935.

Because S.S.S. is a rather unorthodox member of Parliament, and a left-of-center one at that, his opponents sometimes accuse him of being a fellow-traveler. This is nonsense. He is not of the mold of which fellow-travelers are made. Individualists are never fellow-travelers. S.S.S. is a democratic Socialist. He seldom joins the extreme left groups that emerge from time to time inside the Labor Party, when the leadership does not seem Socialist enough for some restless party members. These groups, by the way, usually disappear as a general election approaches.

Though far from being a fellow-traveler, S.S.S. nevertheless advocates an accommodation between East and West and the abolition of the cold war. The trouble is that the Silverman type of politician is so very often let down by both sides.

S.S.S. is a proud Jew, not one of those who try to submerge their Jewishness in socialism. This is why he never had much sympathy for the Bund and always actively supported the Zionist Socialists. Since the split in the Israeli Labor Party, the Mapai, his natural sympathies are with the left-wing Mapam.

Silverman never believed that socialism in itself could solve the Jewish problem, and he advocated a Jewish state from the outset. He once said that as long as the world remained what it was, it would be criminal folly to rely on the instincts of human-ity and justice, or on socialist theory, for the protection of the Jews. This attitude brought him to the World Jewish Congress, where he played a prominent part for many years as chairman of its British Section and as a member of its World Executive. He is still a member of the World Executive, but is no longer active in the British Section.

Suffering humanity in general is Silverman's absorbing interest, but he also has an eye and ear for the needs of the individual. This makes him a good constituency member. He may be difficult to get along with, in some respects being so very argumentative, but when the humble and the poor of his constituency, Nelson and Colne in Lancashire, come to him with their troubles, he does not argue with them, he helps to improve their lot.

In private life this fiery leader is a very relaxed and comfortable citizen, with a nice house in one of London's best residential districts, a wife who shares his political interests and his leisure, and three sons who are receiving an excellent middle-class education and are given the good things of life. S.S.S. can be seen taking his youngest son for a walk on Hampstead Heath on a Sunday morning, tweeds and all; or driving a fast and expensive car into the country. He keeps the Yom Kippur fast and eats matzot on Pesach.

Talk to Silverman and he will tell you that his twenty-eight years in Parliament have been "wasted years." What he means is that he has exercised less influence than he should have. But "he who has done enough for his time has done enough for all time," to quote Schiller. The welfare state, the voluntary freeing of colonies, the changes in some harsh laws — all are the result of a great collective effort over the last quarter of a century, and Silverman has made his contribution to this effort.

S.S.S. has delivered many good speeches in the House, but his best was the one he made during the debate on the arrest of the Jewish Agency leaders. Robert Boothby (now Lord Boothby) described it at the time as the best speech he had ever heard in the House. Even Silverman himself says that it bears re-reading. And the late World Jewish Congress leader, Ben Rubinstein, had the Hansard (official record) volume containing this speech bound in morocco and presented to Silverman's youngest boy, with the advice to read it when he grew up.

I was chatting with Silverman one afternoon in the Member's Bar, where he took me for a drink (soft for both of us).

"Can you imagine yourself getting a peerage?" I asked him.

He laughed his infectious laugh. The idea of Silverman as a lord is really funny. I can't think why one of our more sophisticated comedians does not introduce "Lord Nelson (and Colne)" into a musical.

"But suppose," I persisted, "they did want to make you a *life* peer in order to shut you up, and you did accept — what would you chose as the motto to go on your coat of arms?"

"Never say die!"

This choice retort is typical of Silverman's brand of humor, which, unlike his temperament, is very English. If a brand of humor is the acid test of belonging to an ethnic group, S.S.S. is an Englishman; if temperament is the test, he is a Jew. Actually he is both: the inner man is Jewish and the outer man English.

"Any objections?" S.S.S. would ask.

Vicky
All People Are Funny

THE NAME FITS its owner like a glove. The great cartoonist — one of the greatest of our time — is a small man of dark Semitic appearance, with a bald head framed by a circle of untidy black hair: Vicky.

The master interpreter of the complex English character and deft exploiter of the English idiom in his captions is not English born. He is the son of a Budapest Jewish jeweler who settled in Berlin between the wars. The father was not, however, just a seller of jewelry, but an artist in his own way, as well. He used to design many of the pieces himself. Thus, creative art runs in the family.

Vicky was already drawing cartoons while in Germany, but with the advent of the Nazis he had to find a new home. He was a Jew, a satirist, an articulate anti-Nazi — not the kind of person who could ever come to terms with the New Germany, even though this was long before the scope of the Nazi atrocities was dreamt of.

Where does one go? To Paris? The United States? England? Vicky decided on England because he was attracted by her political freedom and civil liberties. It did not take him long to make his mark. For Vicky is a rare combination of brilliant draughtsman, acute political observer, and sharp social satirist. On top of it all, he has a sense of fun, as distinct from the sense of humor which is taken for granted in a cartoonist.

A poignant cartoon of Vicky's depicting the suffering of a minority or of a subject people may be followed by a light-hearted parody of a famous advertisement; a stinging cartoon underlining the inefficiency of the government — no matter what government, they are all inefficient at times — may be followed by a delightful drawing of a motor show where American cars are trying to impress people by their bigness while French cars are trying to impress people by their smallness.

Juliet Pannett.

It isn't that Vicky is trying to cater to every taste. All people are funny — the important and humble, the rich and the poor, the stupid and the clever — even the cartoonists themselves. Vicky is the first to recognize it. He often puts himself in a corner of his own cartoons — small figure, bald head, lack of trimness in dress, and all. And his cartoon character, Electrovic, is Vicky turned robot by way of bowing to the inevitable and accepting the Robot Age. An electronic machine turning out cartoons — Vicky would not mind at all, provided he was in charge of the machine. One thing he would never do — he would not leave it to his editors.

Editors give him complete freedom, otherwise they cannot have him. For years the now defunct liberal *News Chronicle* was Vicky's home. One day its editors refused to print a cartoon of his — and Vicky handed in his notice. He went to the *Daily Mirror,* a tabloid with the largest morning circulation in the world. The *Mirror* is not a sophisticated paper by any means, but Vicky was given complete freedom there. The *Mirror* has a daily circulation of over four million and reaches about twelve million readers. And there is always the highbrow *New Statesman and Nation,* to which Vicky has been a contributor for many years. So he had no qualms about the move. Now Vicky is with the *Evening Standard,* a conservative paper which gives him complete freedom. He is even permitted to tease Lord Beaverbrook, the redoubtable publisher of the *Standard.*

Vicky is opposed to German rearmament, even today. But there is nothing particularly Jewish in his attitude. He opposes German rearmament — a lost battle — as a man of the world and political scientist, not as a Jew.

Where is Vicky the Jew? In fact, where is the original Victor Weiss of Budapest? Has he renounced his Jewishness like Arthur Koestler, another genius from Budapest who became an Englishman?

Not quite. Vicky, unlike Koestler, was never deeply involved in Zionism or in the struggle for Jewish survival that went on between the wars. There was, consequently, no need for soul searching and nothing to renounce. Vicky is simply a citizen of the world with a British passport who happens to be a Jew and does not mind a bit.

There are prophetic elements in Vicky's sense of mission and his fight for justice. This is Vicky the Jew, but not exclusively so. It was the Jew within that made Vicky go to Israel, and the result was a series of drawings which showed a deep insight into the meaning of Israel. Nothing of the superficial "good luck to them, they do a fine job," but an understanding and grasp of the problems, the lights and shades, the sorrows and joys of Israel, which only a Jew is capable of.

Vicky works at the *Evening Standard* offices, where he has a rather drab studio. The paper can afford something better, of course, but Vicky seems to be happy in the bare room with its drawing board and simple desk. This is where the famous cartoons are born every day. "It is a struggle every time," Vicky told me. Strange for a man with such an easy touch. But then, a conscience is a very hard taskmaster. The 'struggle is inherent in the decision as to what to say. Once this is agreed upon between the master and his conscience, there is no problem about putting it on paper. The master takes over, and the cartoon is born — in no time.

Robert Weltsch

Eternal Values and Daily Journalism

THE NAME OF ROBERT WELTSCH is inseparably connected with the *Juedische Rundschau*, very much as is the name of Henry Wickham Steed with The Times, Kingsley Martin with the New Statesman, Arthur Hays Sulzberger with the New York Times, and J. L. Greenberg with the Jewish Chronicle. But Weltsch would have made his mark in Jewish journalism and letters even if he had not come to Berlin on December 1, 1919, to assume the editorship of that famous weekly. He remains today, twenty-four years after the liquidation of the *Rundschau* by the Nazis, one of the outstanding Jewish journalists and essayists, the London correspondent of *Haaretz,* and the editor of the *Leo Baeck Institute Year Book.*

Robert Weltsch was born on June 20, 1891, in Prague, the son of a lawyer whom Weltsch describes as a faithful Jew but never a Zionist. Robert attended high school in Prague and afterwards the Prague University, where he received his doctorate in law as the First World War broke out. He went straight into the Austro-Hungarian army, was commissioned, and fought on the Russian front. He was demobilized as a lieutenant and never returned to Prague. A Zionist in his student days, he had become a member of Bar-Kochba, an organization which preached cultural Zionism of the Ahad Ha'am and Buber brand, and in 1913 published a collection of essays edited by him and Hans Kohn which created a lively discussion in the Zionist movement. Now he was attracted to the Zionist centre of Vienna. Herzl's city, where he was appointed editor of the *Juedische Zeitung* and General Secretary of the Juedischer Nationalrat (Jewish National Council). Soon afterwards he accepted the invitation of the Zionist organization in Germany to become editor of the *Juedische Rundschau* (Jewish Review). Except for a one-year period in 1923-24, which Weltsch spent in London at the invitation of Chaim Weizmann, he edited the journal until September, 1938. Weltsch left Germany when there was no prospect of keeping the *Rundschau* alive much

Juliet Pannett.

longer. Soon he was in Jerusalem. He is now an Israeli citizen,
of course, and writes in Hebrew as well as in English and German.

The *Juedische Rundschau* had been in existence since 1895,
and by the time Weltsch took over the editorship, it had acquired
a reputation as a solid, informative, and nicely printed Zionist
weekly. Under him it continued to be the mouthpiece of German
Zionism and one of the best *Golah* journals, but Weltsch gave it a
new spirit and made of it much more than merely a good journal
of a great movement: he infused it with his own brand of Zionism
and his liberal political outlook; it bore the stamp of his own
humanism and humanity. The influence of the *Rundschau* spread
beyond the frontiers of Germany, to the German-speaking countries of Central Europe and to Poland and the Baltic states, where
German was the language of the West and the vehicle of Western
culture, until Hitler made an end to the journal. All through the
years, Weltsch put much stress on education and cultural activity
in general and preached a policy of neighborly friendship and
understanding towards the Arabs of Palestine. His vision was that
of a Jewish National Home based upon co-operation between the
country's Jews and Arabs.

Looking at the state of affairs today, Robert Weltsch describes
his expectation of Jewish-Arab co-operation for the purpose of
establishing some sort of joint state as "perhaps quixotic." And
so it was, but only in the sense in which "Love thy neighbor" is
quixotic, and world peace and disarmament are quixotic. We may
be forced to deviate from these ideals in the throes of a struggle
for survival, and for lack of response by the other side, but love
of our fellow human beings remains an ideal to strive for, and
those who preach it are still the salt of the earth.

When Hitler came to power in January of 1933, Weltsch remained at his post. In his inimitable style, and with great skill,
he managed to report the Nazi iniquities and to criticize Hitler's
government, to plead for reason and humanity and, at the same
time, to sustain the spirit of his Jewish readers. The art of the
Juedische Rundschau in those days consisted of resisting the Nazi
onslaught with great determination, though in a form which did
not give justification for police interference. This was "the language of the persecuted," proud and firm, but somehow camou-
flaged, often ironical. Weltsch's Czech passport enabled him to
travel abroad, but it afforded no protection for his journal. Time
and again the *Rundschau* was confiscated or closed down, and
Weltsch had to go and plead with the Nazi authorities to let it

come out again. In view of what we know about the Nazi horrors of later years, it may seem incredible, but time and again they permitted the *Rundschau* to resume publication — until November, 1938, when all was finished. It is noteworthy that many non-Jews used to buy the journal in that period; it was the only anti-Nazi paper *publicly* sold until 1936.

On April 4, 1933, there appeared Weltsch's editorial, *"Tragt ihn mit Stolz, den gelben Fleck"* (Wear the Yellow Badge with Pride). In it he called upon German Jews to fall back upon their inner strength and to find succor and hope for a better future in the Jewish past and Jewish teachings. Here was a man guiding a bewildered generation and teaching it to answer a challenge in terms of eternal values which could not be obliterated by the might of the Nazi legions. It remains a landmark in the history of European Jewry. Weltsch himself would say that he could not, in retrospect, accept the praise often bestowed on his particular article. After what has happened since that day, he will say, as he once told me, that the notion of wearing the yellow badge with pride is almost unbearable. In April, 1933, the yellow badge represented a humiliation, and Jews could react to it with an inner pride at being Jews, a defiance of their oppressors. A few years later, this badge was used to mark people out for extermination. That is why Weltsch does not like that famous article now. However, this kind of piece must be judged by the response of those to whom it was addressed *at the time.* To them it was the elixir of life.

From the viewpoint of sheer writing, perhaps Weltsch did write better essays and articles in that period. One was penned on the 150th anniversary of Lessing's *Nathan der Weise,* in 1933. Weltsch used this occasion to assert the faith of a humanist in the face of the Nazi orgy of violence and inhumanity. While expressing abhorrence of Nazi brutality, he acknowledged the messages of condolence and friendship that had reached him from gentiles inside Germany, and which saved his faith in humanity. This firm belief in humanity he still retains. He took it with him to Palestine, where he found an outlet in the *Ichud* movement of Dr. J. L. Magnes. This was an élite that preached co-operation with the Arabs. It included men like Moshe Smilanski, Reb Binyamin, Martin Buber, Ernst Simon, Werner Senator, Norman Bentwich. The cards were stacked against them. In the Arab camp the Mufti gained ascendancy; the Jews had to react with force in order to preserve the *Yishuv;* and the British, prompted as they were by a short-sighted policy, did not encourage co-operation between the two races in Palestine.

Despite the Arab reaction to the partition resolution of the U.N. Assembly passed on November 29, 1947, which together with the subsequent war of independence left no room for a body like the *Ichud,* its surviving members continue to preach their basic idea. They retain the grudging affection even of violent activists among the Israelis. For such activism is not an article of faith with these Israelis, but only a strategy of survival. Weltsch himself has spent most of the time following the establishment of the State of Israel in London, and has taken no active part in Israeli politics since.

Today, at seventy, Robert Weltsch, a small figure who looks larger than he is thanks to a distinguished head, a man of great charm, and with the perfect manners of a nineteenth century intellectual, conveys an impression of tolerant detachment. He looks upon the antics of our generation with amused pity, and has not given up trying to make us mend our ways. Five of the *Leo Baeck Institute Year Books* — each a volume of over four hundred pages — have already appeared under his editorship. The purpose of these monumental books is to give modern readers an idea of the intellectual, cultural, and economic achievements of German Jewry and — most importantly — an opportunity to acquaint themselves with the brand of Jewish philosophy that evolved in Germany and made its impact on Jewish thought and action all over the world.

Weltsch finds escape and relaxation in music. He often complains of being "tired," but he really means disappointed. No wonder. The world constantly fails to live up to his standards.

Isaac Wolfson

A Tycoon in Arba Kanfot

THE AMERICANS, with their flair for arresting terminology, have dug up the name *tycoon* for the head of a large business enterprise or industrial combine. The term has come to stay on both sides of the Atlantic, even though respectable English dictionaries still confine themselves to the original definition of this entry. A tycoon was, of course, the Shogun or commander-in-chief of the Japanese army and the temporal ruler of Japan until about the middle of the nineteenth century. Now the order of things in Japan has changed, as we all know, and there is no room for confusion — a tycoon is a modern large-scale operator in the spheres of finance, business, industry, and the like.

The public image of a tycoon is easily definable: He sits in a sumptuous, close-carpeted office looking down over the rooftops of lesser men, with an original Renoir on the wall facing him, and a photograph of his current wife at his left elbow. His desk is immense, glass-topped, and devoid of any papers or books; on it are only three telephones of different colors and an intercom for direct communication with secretaries and flunkies. A tycoon speaks on two telephones simultaneously and still manages to bark orders into the intercom as well. Very few tycoons possess Napoleon's gift of speaking to two people and reading a document at the same time. But the system works, because the people a tycoon speaks to are dependent upon him and so keep on saying yes-yes-yes. I remember once telling a tycoon that I liked to have the undivided attention of a man I talk to. He was a little shaken, but soon recovered sufficiently to tell his secretary that he was not to be disturbed and gave me his full attention, saying: "Well, what else can I do with you? You are not employed by me, nor do you want to do business with me."

This, then, is a tycoon. One should perhaps add that at certain times of the year hordes of tycoons descend upon certain fashionable holiday resorts, and there they play together, like whales in Artic waters.

Sir Isaac Wolfson is a tycoon by any definition, yet he does not conform to the pattern in every detail. But let us first establish his claim to the designation.

The Great Universal Stores Limited, of which Sir Isaac is chairman and managing director, is a group of companies dealing through hundreds of stores and other establishments in furniture, clothing, household goods, textiles, and most other things which people in the affluent society buy, whether they really need them or not. Sir Isaac was a pioneer in the mail order business in the United Kingdom. He now also controls some enterprises in the Commonwealth, in Israel, and in other countries.

The Great Universal Stores are known by their initials, G.U.S., hence the popular name of the G.U.S. shares — "Gusies." Most of the shares are held by Sir Isaac himself or by members of his family. In 1952 the G.U.S. had a profit of 8,638,047 pounds sterling, on which 5,365,365 pounds in taxes was paid, which still left about three and a half million pounds net profit. The assets of the group in that year were 21,527,186 pounds. Since then there has been a steady rise in profits and assets, scarcely affected by the economic recessions of the past decade. In 1961 gross profits amounted to 26,066,113 pounds, taxes to 13,913,448 pounds, and assets to 106,592,324 pounds.

Take-over men are very common nowadays. Everybody seeks to take over everybody else — from giant combines trying to take over other combines of similar size to the suburban butcher who tries to take over his competitor and run a "chain" of two butcher shops. But Sir Isaac was one of the original take-over men in Britain.

Some people still speak with nostalgia about the independent shop where they and their parents and grandparents before them did their shopping. But then, some people are also apt to become sentimental about the original railways with their steam engines and soot-covered firemen. Given the society we live in, take-overs are on the whole beneficial to the customers. In the case of Sir Isaac Wolfson, he seems to be aware of the fact that some people still have original minds and individual tastes, and can still afford to indulge them. Some of the stores within his group bear famous names and cater to special customers. Those he left as they were — he did not vulgarize them after the take-over. In some other cases he gave the former owners shares in his group, made them junior partners, appointed them directors or managers, included them in his entourage, and introduced more drive and efficiency into the stores thus taken over. The twenty-six million pounds

Juliet Pannett.

in profits for 1961 bear witness to the success of these operations.

Isaac Wolfson was made a baronet in the New Year's Honors List of 1962. He is now styled as "Sir Isaac," without the surname, when addressed directly or referred to; his wife Edith is now Lady Wolfson; his son Leonard will one day inherit the title. The citation says that Sir Isaac was made a baronet "for philanthropic services." This is a true description of the reason for the honor. He is one of the few great philanthropists in Britain, both in scope and in mode of giving.

In 1955, the Isaac Wolfson Foundation was established to centralize his charitable activities and to provide continuous grants to various good causes out of the earned income on the capital assigned by the endower for this purpose. This is the chosen method of the begetters of the great foundations bearing such names as Rockefeller, Ford, and Nuffield. In this respect, the Americans have shown the way.

Britain is, of course, a welfare state — in many ways a trailblazer for, and an example to, other welfare states. The state takes care of the basic needs of its citizens and residents — educates their children, looks after their health, supports them in times of sickness or unemployment, and helps to provide cheaper housing for lower income groups. "From the cradle to the grave" is not an empty phrase, and yet the gap between the rich and the poor remains wide. There was a time when the founding fathers of the welfare state believed that there would be no room in it for individual charity, or for private initiative in the advancement of scientific research. It seemed simple: the state would take all the taxes available and supply all the needs existing.

In practice it had not worked out that way. Those who planned the welfare state could not have forseen that fifteen years after the war countries would still have to spend gigantic sums on arms; nor did they estimate correctly the cost of the welfare state. As it is, there is in Britain, as in any welfare state, a constant competition between priorities, all of them vital. Even priorities have to take their turn, as Churchill once put it in his own inimitable way.

And so there is room for private initiative in the field of charity and in the promotion of science and the arts. Such private endeavors complement the work of the welfare state, and it would be difficult to imagine its course without them. In fact, they have increased both in numbers and scope since the welfare state came into being in Britain.

The Isaac Wolfson Foundation, like all his operations, is designed on a large scale. It is based on the adage, which he takes quite seriously, that a man who amasses a large fortune is but its trustee, and that he should use at least part of it for the improvement of the human condition. Beween the day of its establishment and the end of 1961, the Isaac Wolfson Foundation distributed 14,340,000 pounds. A list of some of its beneficiaries will give an idea of its scope and aims: a quarter of a million pounds to the Westminster Hospital in London; another quarter of a million pounds to London University; a hundred and fifty thousand pounds to the British Empire Cancer Campaign; a hundred and twenty-five thousand pounds to the Post-graduate School of Medicine; three hundred thousand pounds to the University of Glasgow; three hundred and fifty thousand pounds to the Imperial College of Science and Technology.

These are very large sums, even by international standards. Smaller amounts were given to the universities of Oxford and Cambridge; to a London school bearing the name of Solomon Wolfson, Sir Isaac's father; to two synagogues, and to many other institutions.

Various donations to Israel are not included in this list; they are provided outside of the Foundation. There is Heichal Shlomo, a religious center — and another memorial to the father of Sir Isaac — which was built entirely on funds provided by Wolfson. There are also large donations to the Weizmann Institute and to Youth Aliyah.

In his commercial activities in Israel Sir Isaac is very much the businessman. He acquired *Paz,* the petroleum distribution company, to take over the Shell installations when that company was about to leave Israel, and he is not losing on it. He also participates in an Israeli investment company which is doing well. In short, he behaves in Israel like so many good Diaspora Jews: he is devoted to the country, extols its achievements, feels at home there, hobnobs with members of the Government, donates large sums — and does some business..

Sir Isaac Wolfson's origins are humble. He was born in Glasgow, Scotland, in 1897. His father was an immigrant from Eastern Europe, who made a bare living. Isaac went to *Cheder* (religious classes) and to a local school. At fourteen he left school and went to work. Starting in furniture, he soon turned to gold whatever he touched. What he knows today he learned himself; he does not claim to know very much, but he can read a balance sheet very well indeed. However, this is not the most important thing; what matters more is his touch, his "sixth sense," which guides him in his social life as much as in his business.

The bedrock of his personality is his Jewishness. He is a "Jewish Jew" with deep Jewish roots, a warden of a synagogue, where he actually prays on the Sabbath and on Jewish holidays. He feels completely at ease only among Jews and speaks with real enthusiasm only about Israel. When he is not engaged in his business, he stays at home and reads a book or goes to the cinema; he has no interest in high society, where his fame and his money would easily give him entrée. His personal friends are all Jews.

There are *Mezuzot* not only on the doors of Isaac Wolfson's private residence but also on the doors of his business head-quarters in Central London. The food at Universal House, the head office of the G.U.S., is strictly kosher. His non-Jewish business associates seem to respect him the more for it.

At home, Wolfson puts on his *Tefilin* every morning for the morning prayer. He goes to synagogue on Friday nights as well as on Saturday mornings. Lady Wolfson lights the candles on Sabbath eve.

Sir Isaac still speaks with a Glasgow accent, though his English is otherwise good, which cannot be said about the English of many Anglo-Jews of his generation.

Sir Isaac is shortish, dark, and broad-shouldered, with thick, greying hair and a strong and finely-featured face. He dresses carefully but not ostentatiously. He is friendly, and his liking for people is genuine. If he sometimes seems aloof, it is due to shyness.

In England, Sir Isaac Wolfson is the classical example, the archetype, of a Jew who is not a formal Zionist — he is not even a member of the Zionist Federation — yet is utterly devoted to Israel. He is the Appeal Chairman of the United Israel Appeal and gives this office a good deal of his time and attention. When he goes to America, he participates in the campaigns of the Israel Appeal there, in order to study the American methods. His technique is now partly American: he knows exactly how much a contributor could give without injury to himself, and he demands that much. He will tell a contributor publicly at the annual Appeal dinner: "Surely you can do better than that!" — and get an increased contribution on the spot. The wonderment at the existence of a Jewish state has never left him, and he gives it expression in public. What would sound trite with a more sophisticated speaker, has the ring of a sincere and genuine *Shehecheyanu,* a thanksgiving to the Almighty for a miracle, when uttered by a man like Sir Isaac. He has neither the cant nor the slickness of the politician, and this makes him so acceptable.

Sir Isaac Wolfson is known among big businessmen as a tycoon with a social conscience. When the British Government asked for a pause in the rise of earnings and profits, to try to catch up with production, the Great Universal Stores was the first large group to restrict dividends by paying less than the profits warranted. This, of course, increased the assets. Good businessmen don't lose by being good citizens, but few of them understand it.

When I spoke to Sir Isaac after his knighthood, he mused: "It is nice to be honored, of course. Remember what Adlai Stevenson has said, 'a little flattery does no harm provided you don't inhale it.' I am trying not to inhale it." And then: "Don't look upon me as sitting on a financial Olympus. I am still the same Isaac Wolfson. My favorite Biblical story is the one about Joseph, who identified himself to his brothers by his name and did not mention titles and status. There is a moral in it."

Whereupon Sir Isaac pulled out his shirt and showed me his *Arba Kanfot* under it. "Why not. The *Goyim* wear a cross next to their skin," he demanded. Really, why not.

This was not an interview, just a chat in the paneled office of the chairman at Universal House. Wolfson mentioned that he was going to be sixty-five soon, and I asked him what he hoped for now, were there any ambitions left.

"Yes," he said, "yes, there is one. I hope and pray that after sixty-five I may be vouchsafed to give to charity and good causes two million pounds every year. This is something worth working for, is it not?"

HE DEVELOPMENT OF ISRAEL presents a kind of topsy-turvy pattern, and it would have been totally untenable but for the fact that it works. They had a university long before they evolved a network of kindergartens, primary schools, and high schools. They had a great trade union movement long before they embarked on the industrialization of the country. They won a war before they had a regular army.

Yigael Yadin is a product of this development. He was born in 1917, the son of E. L. Sukenik, the noted archeologist. He attended high school in Jerusalem and joined the Haganah in his teens. Before he was thirty, he rose to be chief of its planning and implementation section. At the outbreak of the War of Independence, he was chief of operations. Thus he was the obvious choice for the post of Chief of Staff of the Israeli Defense Forces when the national army was created. This post he held from 1947 until the end of 1952.

Under his leadership the army won the war and established the firm foundation upon which the state could develop. It was also under Yadin that the army was molded into the fighting force it is today and, no less important, also became an instrument of education, both in the narrow sense, and in the wider sense of molding the young men and women from various diasporas and different Jewish backgrounds into sons and daughters of the State of Israel. At thirty-five, Yigael Yadin was a retired major-general, the highest rank in the Israeli Defense Forces, an an ex-Chief of Staff. He was free to pursue his chosen vocation — archeology.

The victor of the War of Independence, a military leader with élan and a profound knowledge of the art of war, has never been to a military academy. Nor did he serve in the British Army during the Second World War, as many of his fellow-officers in the Israeli Defense Forces did. He became a general as the Haganah became an army, the Jewish Agency Executive a govern-

Juliet Pannett.

Ygael Yadin

ment, and the *Yishuv* a nation. And he was none the worse for
it. His was not a courtesy title, as are military titles given sometimes to leaders of victorious independence movements. Yadin
knew all about the business of training and fighting before the
dignity and status of a general were conferred on him. He soon
proved it conclusively.

In his service days Yadin was of the type known as an intellectual general, a military leader who relates fighting to wider
issues and sees it as an unavoidable necessity in certain circumstances, a means to an end and not a destiny in itself. This
type of military leader is not unknown in America and England.
Perhaps the late General George Marshall in America and
Lord Mountbatten in England are good examples. A word of
warning is necessary here: Intellectual generals must not be confused with political generals; they have no politics while they
wear their uniform.

Yadin retired from active service because, he says, he felt he
had made his contribution and it was time to turn the responsibilities over to people capable of carrying on where he left off.
There was also the lure of archeology, of course, and he felt the
time had come to devote himself to it without other distractions.
The power to make a decision, an important quality in any
military leader, asserted itself here, too. A man with less tenacity
of purpose might have carried on for a few more years, and have
become a frustrated archeologist. Yadin cut himself loose from
the Defense Forces in time, exchanged the usual letters of regret
and appreciation with the prime minister, and went back to his
books and field work.

Yadin's absorption with the past influenced his strategic thinking and his battle tactics during his tenure of office as Chief of
Staff. He has said many times that the nature of warfare in Israel
has not changed since biblical times.

Talking to Yadin recently, I had a chance to ask him to re-
examine this concept from the distance of fourteen years after
the War of Independence and eight years after the Sinai campaign.
Yadin now is far removed from the day-to-day problems of the
Israeli Defense Forces, and his discourse has a purely theoretical
character.

"This propostion may not be valid for other countries in relation
to their experience," he said, "but it is valid in the specific conditions of Israel. It must also be remembered that it holds good
for land warfare only, which, however, still plays a decisive role

in local encounters. The geography has not changed since biblical days, though the landscape may have done so; nor have the enemies changed in regard to both their location and their aims. In the War of Independence and in the Sinai campaign, battles were fought almost on the very sites of the biblical battles, and so the experience of our ancestors could serve as a guide. What is no less important, this knowledge that ancient Jews have fought battles on the same spots has a mystical effect on the soldiers; it is a morale builder."

From this the conversation turned to the prophetic sayings about danger from the North, the unreliability of Egypt, and so on. "The prophets," said Yadin, "were diplomats of a high order, perhaps the first diplomats, in our sense, that the Jewish people had. Their appraisal of a politico-military situation was invariably accurate and incisive. Sometimes the danger from the North was greater; at other times Egypt threatened Israel more imminently. The problem was where to be more on the alert — and it still is."

Archeology was in the Yadin family. "The atmosphere at home was permeated with archeology," says Yadin. But there was also the personal inclination. His brother, Yossef, also grew up in the same atmosphere — and became an actor. Yigael chose archeology deliberately. After leaving the army, he went back to his studies and within two years gained his Ph.D. at the Hebrew University.

Like Yadin the general, Yadin the archeologist is also Israel-trained. He has worked abroad for lengthy periods, especially in England, but he has never actually studied at a foreign university. Today his time is divided between teaching — he is a professor at the Hebrew University — and archeological expeditions during vacations. Yigael's humanity, fluency, and eagerness to explain and impart knowledge, along with his humor, often so lighthearted as to border on simple, clean fun, make him a great teacher. But his world renown is bound up with his archeological explorations and his interpretations of their finds.

Archeological expeditions are often referred to as "campaigns." And there is, in fact, a similarity between the preparations, as far as logistics are concerned. Yadin's experience as a soldier is very valuable in his present vocation. He also has an uncanny feel for the past, a kind of sixth sense. This helps in fixing the sites for "digs" and in the deciphering and interpreting of his finds.

Those great non-Jewish archeologists who uncovered the past in the Middle East, Greece, and elsewhere, have proved that you don't have to be native to the place in order to do so. Yet, as you read Yadin's books and articles, and even more so as you talk to him, you somehow feel that his Jewishness is decisive in his achievements in archeology. Only a man born and nurtured in Jerusalem, to whom the Bible in its Hebrew original is not only an open book but part of his very being, and who is so well integrated into the present-day life of Israel, can achieve Yadin's degree of empathy with every era he has dug up. Some people disagree with this view, I know. But could it be argued reasonably that a non-Jewish archeologist would *understand* the commander of a Jewish army of eighteen hundred years ago as well as the archeologist does who was himself the Chief of Staff of the Israeli Defense Forces in a war fought on the same terrain?

Yadin's name is bound up with Hazor, the Dead Sea Scrolls, and the Bar Kochba Letters. Hazor, in Galilee, has yielded important finds of great significance to biblical scholars and historians. The Hazor expedition, which lasted three seasons, was an orthodox archeological enterprise, though perhaps directed by Yadin with more personal application and a greater sense of kinship with the place than would have been the case if it were led by an outsider. Hazor is the biblical city mentioned in Joshua ("head of all those kingdoms"), Judges, (Jabin was the King of Hazor, and his captain was Sisera), I Kings, (King Solomon rebuilt it together with Megiddo and Gezer), II Kings, (in the days of King Pekah, Tiglathpileser III conquered it, together with a large slice of the country — in 732 B.C.E.). It is also mentioned in pre-biblical Egyptian documents. Hazor finds were later exhibited in the British Museum. We now have a clearer understanding of the historical periods reflected in the ancient cities built one upon the ruins of the other.

The romantic story of the first four Dead Sea Scrolls, their acquisition by Yadin in America, with the help of a Jewish philanthropist, their deciphering, and the subsequent search for more scrolls in the area of the Dead Sea has fired the imagination of millions, and this popular interest has not waned. The interest of the scrolls to scholars is, briefly, this: They are the Bible scrolls of the Essenes, who withdrew to the desert around the Dead Sea at about 100 B.C.E. Thus, these scrolls are about a thousand years older than the hitherto known Hebrew texts of the Bible from which current translations have been made. Apart from any possible corrections to the known texts, the scrolls also yield completely new passages, unknown before.

Yadin's book on the Dead Sea Scrolls, *The War of the Sons of Light on the Sons of Darkness,* has become a best seller in its class. A new English edition has recently been published by the Oxford University Press.

The Bar Kochba Letters, the yield of another expedition directed by Yadin, shed new light on the Bar Kochba insurrection. Yadin himself considers this last find the most important. I quote him: "Hazor is valuable to Bible scholars and historians of the seventeenth to sixth centuries B.C.E. It is not sensational. We had an idea what to expect. It is important in a way; it satisfies our natural curiosity about ancient civilizations; but there is nothing world-shaking about these finds. The first Dead Sea Scrolls give us a better understanding of the Bible. There is still a great deal of research to be done, by myself and others, on Hazor and on the Bible scrolls. But the truly sensational find, of a nature that will give us a new appreciation of a crucial period in Jewish and, incidentally, world history, is the Bar Kochba Letters. These are from the period of the second century A.D. — the Bar Kochba insurrection lasted from the years 132 to 135, of which we knew very little. We had only limited sources for our knowledge about the Jewish condition at the time, and here we have before us a new wealth of material — including the dispatches of Shimon Bar Kochba himself!"

The excitement of Yadin over this find is infectious. A change of accepted notions of history is always exciting — and disturbing. We are inclined "to hold what we have" unless we are forced to revise our ideas by documentary evidence.

The man who found and deciphered the Bar Kochba Letters was seated before me in his London apartment, wearing an open-necked maroon sports shirt, and chatting amiably. He has the ability to throw light on an ancient civilization in a couple of pointed sentences.

Yadin's next expedition will be to Massada, the great fortress on the Dead Sea, which was the scene of so much historical drama in the days of Herod, and later in the Bar Kochba insurrection. "We have done some probing, but we must soon get down to the real business of digging."

Archeological expeditions are very expensive enterprises. Hazor, for example, was made possible by James A. de Rothschild, "whose great enthusiasm and generosity turned the excavation from a dream into a reality," to quote Yadin. The Government of Israel is ever ready to help. And there is the enthusiastic voluntary labor of member of kibbutzim and students, as well as the invaluable services of the Defense Forces.

Archeology has a strange fascination for us. It also has its practical application: By knowing more of the past we are better equipped to cope with the present. Great archeologists are invariably regarded with a mixture of awe and affection. It is in a way a clue to the basic character of the Israelis that Yigael Yadin has earned in his own country more admiration and affection with his archeological victories than he did with his victories against the Arabs.